WILL TO LIVE:
A SAGA OF SURVIVAL

By Gary Edinger

WITH A FOREWORD BY DON BURGESS

WILL TO LIVE: A SAGA OF SURVIVAL

By Gary Edinger

Foreword by Don Burgess

Copyright 2010 by Gary Edinger

ISBN 1-931291-81-0

Library of Congress Control Number: 2010936463

Published in the United States of America

First Edition

STONEYDALE PRESS PUBLISHING COMPANY
523 Main Street • P.O. Box 188
Stevensville, Montana 59870
Phone: 406-777-2729
Email: stoneydale@montana.com

ACKNOWLEDGMENTS

I would like to thank Don Burgess for helping to edit this book and for writing the Foreword. Thanks also to the publisher, Dale Burk, for being so easy to work with. Thank you to all my family and friends, past and present, for your support and for helping to shape my life. This book is dedicated to all those who chose a profession to help others in time of need, sometimes risking their own lives in the process. In particular, Price County Deputies Joanne Heitkemper and Brian Roush, EMT volunteers Bryan Curtis, Mike Tyrrell, Dave Chamberlain and Jim Cejka from the Central Price County Ambulance Service and helicopter transport paramedics Nancy Casey and David Martin. They all helped to save my life that day.

Thanks also to Dr. Leggon and Dr. Bibbo and their staff at St. Joseph's Hospital in Marshfield, who didn't think they could save my knee but wanted to try – and did it! A final thank you to my case manager from the insurance company, Monica Skubal, who fought to make sure insurance paid for the best of care. Although many encouraged me to write this book, Monica's words were the ones that convinced me my story was special and I needed to tell it.

FOREWORD

When Gary Edinger approached me about writing a foreword for his book, I said I would be honored. From the first time I met him I knew he was someone special because of our shared passion for a special place: the Bitterroot Mountains.

The stretch of the Bitterroots that marks the state line west of my home in Montana's Bitterroot Valley, and east of Idaho's Selway River, comprises some of the roughest, most inhospitable terrain in the Lower 48. It's just about as wild and wooly as it gets.

It's beautiful when you see it in the right light, the right frame of mind. But it's rough country for the traveler, especially if you venture far from the mainline Forest Service trails, and it can turn on you—darken your day in a heartbeat. It's the kind of country only hardy, woods-wise, self-sufficient people should tackle. That's why it's not surprising that some parts of it see no man-tracks from year to year. No people at all except for a guy named Gary Edinger and one or two companions he's persuaded to go in deep with him.

Word came down from that range a few years ago of this wiry cheerful middle-aged man traipsing through the backcountry carrying a towering canvas-wrapped pack that appeared to weigh as much as he did. A former colleague at *Bugle* magazine, himself an intrepid wilderness wanderer, bumped into the guy on one of his solo excursions among the Selway-Bitterroot's trackless ramparts. The two of them struck up an acquaintance, and not much later a manuscript with Gary's byline appeared on my desk at the Rocky Mountain Elk Foundation headquarters in Missoula. Turns out the guy could also write. His story of a truly grueling elk hunt in the Selway-Bitterroot brought back vivid memories of hellacious hunts of my own in some of that same country, and we published it in a special section called "Big Weather." It's a story that will tell you a lot about grit and determination, and you can read it here in this collection of stories from the life of an extraordinary man.

Gary grew up in Wisconsin's backwoods in the 1950s. It might as well have been the 1850s. Electricity and other conveniences were slow to arrive in that part of the world, and folks were still strictly square dancing long after Elvis arrived. Cows and horses, saws and axes, woodstoves and woodpiles, guns and traps and fishing poles were common and crucial elements of life. Hardship, toil and free-ranging self-reliance kept alive a pioneer frontiersman-like spunk and vigor rarely seen these days. And something more: a quiet sense of humor and humility that often marks individuals of uncommon strength and courage and force of will.

Those qualities define Gary Edinger, who could have served with distinction with Hillary on Everest, Shackleton in the Antarctic, Lewis and Clark on the Missouri and the Columbia. A truly free man, Gary has always operated under his own terms, making his living by his wit and determination and the strength of his arms and legs. A very high-energy individual, he's perpetually hunting, fishing, cutting timber, writing, building, tending his livestock, being a good husband and father, calling square dances, traveling back and forth between Wisconsin and the Bitterroot Mountains in Montana and Idaho, and fighting to protect wild places and the overall quality of life in his neighborhood and beyond.

Maybe you've heard that old saying, "as busy as a one-legged man in a kicking contest." It's a particularly fitting way to describe Gary, who has been, since 2007, literally a one-legged man, and is now engaged in what amounts to a kicking contest of his own devising. Since losing the lower half of his left leg in a logging accident, he's set out to prove, just as he's done all his life, that he can still do whatever he sets his mind on doing. If you read carefully enough, you will gain insights into how his mind works and the unique ways he can summon his sheer force of will to overcome insurmountable odds. After you have finished this book you will have been entertained by his stories and inspired by his triumphs.

Don Burgess
Former *Bugle* hunting editor
Florence, Montana August, 2010

TABLE OF CONTENTS

Preface

It was February 15, 2007, about 5:30 in the morning when Leanne came into the bedroom to wake me up. She said, "You're not going to work are you? It's 40 below zero." It was more a statement than a question. I work as a self-employed independent logger; liking the hard work outdoors and the freedom and independence it gives me. After thirty years of being married, Leanne knows better than to try and tell me I can't do something. It only makes me more determined. I know it's a character flaw that can work for or against a person.

Rightfully, she worries about me, knowing how dangerous my job is, especially working alone. If something happened and I wasn't killed outright, we both knew it wouldn't take long for the extreme cold to finish the job. I always try to reassure her by telling her, "I've come home to you every night, haven't I?"

Most normal loggers won't work when it's colder than minus 10; too hard on equipment and on you. But there is nothing normal about me. Sure, I have a wife, two fine kids, a house and a pickup, but that's where normal ends. Once I went to work when it was 45 below and stuck it out all day, even though it never got above minus 20, just to see if I could do it. For some reason, I always have to push things. Perhaps a shrink would say that I'm afraid. Afraid that if I quit this one time, then it will be even easier to quit the next time.

The things I've done so far in my fifty-five years were not normal either. I've raced sled dogs, been a commercial salmon fisherman on the Yukon River in Alaska, an elk hunting guide and a log cabin builder. I've done everything I wanted to and if I died tomorrow, there would be no regrets. It seems like I'm always looking for a challenge, and finding that the greatest rewards come from doing things the hard way.

My family has a Ph.D. in doing things the hard way. Great-Grandpa and Grandma Edinger were the first pioneers to settle along the lower reaches of the North Fork of the Jump River, which became part of the Kennan Township of Price County in northern Wisconsin. As the family grew, relatives naturally spread out along the river. The perseverance and tenacity it took to build their homes and tame the raw land, trying to eke out an existence, led to a sense of accomplishment and self-esteem. There is a family pride in that. That pride comes naturally for me from having over 100 years of deep roots on the same land and listening to their stories of overcoming an unforgiving environment. The importance to pass on that heritage runs deep inside me and gives me a sense of pride I feel no need to apologize for.

That Edinger tenacity was certainly part of why I had to go to work that morning; to do something others wouldn't. I couldn't let the cold beat me. The challenge had to be met. I knew by the time I drove the one and a half hours to my job east of Phillips and got my diesel skidder warmed up and started, the temperature would be tolerable. Had I known what waited for me in the woods that day, I would have gladly stayed in bed. After that day, even if I ever wanted to, I would never ever have the chance to be normal again.

Chapter 1

ALONE, WITH A HALF-HOUR TO LIVE

When the tree hit there was no pain, just a big jolt, a shock through my whole system. I'd felt that once before when I was a little kid. I was learning to ice skate on the river when I fell backwards and slammed my head on the ice, hard! It felt like my whole body was numb, only that time I knew where I was hit.

I ended up sitting astraddle another tree I had just cut. My first reaction was to touch my chest with my right hand. "Oh, I'm alright," I thought to myself. As I went to stand up, my left leg didn't touch the ground. I tried harder the second time, feeling my thigh move, but still my foot did not feel the frozen, snow-covered ground.

As I was bringing my eyes around to see what the problem was, my brain was preparing me to expect a broken leg. What I saw instead sent wave after wave of horror and panic washing over me. Just below my knee I had no leg! It was gone! Sheared right off! Through the steam rising off the end of my stump, I could see a stream of red hot blood the size of a pencil arcing down. Then I spotted my foot, lying there twisted backward on the red snow, staring back at me out of the top of my pac boot. No, No, NO! It can't be! Wake up from this dream! Please, go back! Do it over! NO! NO!!

Then, just like throwing a switch, my training took over – training from years of hunting and camping, living and working in the natural world, mostly in wild places and often alone. What I have witnessed and accepted is how the natural world can sometimes be cruel and always final: trees struck by lightning and windstorms, heavy rains and snowfalls, animals killing other animals. And myself killing. In nature there is no such thing as compromise. These things are final. There is no going back. It came to me, "You've got to get going here." So, just like that, I accepted it. My leg was gone. It's done! Now what? I've learned to mentally have plans for the what-ifs. You have to when you're alone far from help in the backcountry. Plan A in the case of a bad chainsaw cut was a tourniquet, so I grabbed both sides of my thigh, swung it over the log, and slid down onto the ground. My boot drug along because it was still attached by some shreds of clothing. The fear was stalking hard inside of me but action seemed to keep it at bay. I grabbed my belt, put it around my leg above the knee and gave it a reef. Between the age of my belt and the adrenaline powering thru my veins the leather could not stand the strain and broke. Quick, Plan B!

You learn to make up a Plan B in the backcountry. The weather changes, the wind changes, the horse goes lame or you go lame, the lead cow goes down instead of up. Lots of things. With sixteen sled dogs on the line I'd learned to solve problems quickly under pressure. Based on following the blood trail of mortally wounded deer, I figured a half hour was all I had. I had to stop my life from leaking out the bottom of my leg to have any chance! Help was a long way away, so what else could I do but tie the damn thing back together and try it again? Fifteen degrees below zero and my fingers felt like stubs as I tried the second time to get a knot that would hold. Once again around my leg, I gave it another reef. I couldn't go easy – I had lots of clothes and muscle to squeeze off. This time I jerked it right off the buckle! *I realized then I was going to die.* A feeling of deepest despair and resignation settled over me. I felt the darkness closing in. For a second and a half I quit. The words formed in my mind; "The heck with it. Just lay back and get cold."

As I settled back on my elbows and stared blankly at the sky, out of nowhere unspoken words came to me. *"What the heck! Why don't you see how far you can get?"* The thought came naturally. After all, it seemed like I had spent most of my life doing that, as had my ancestors.

I realize now that simple little thought, "Why don't you see how far you can get?" was my way of sucking it up, of summoning all of my strengths. My strengths came from being part of a large family group of self-reliant, rugged outdoorsmen, of a genetic makeup I was born with and a rich life few others had the resolve to experience and sometimes endure. My life of fifty-five years was now at the peak of the pyramid with my genetic makeup as a base, the culture of the community I had been raised in and my life's lessons filling in everything else. In the next half hour I would need it all.

Chapter 2

THE FAMILY

From the beginning I was proud of being an Edinger. I don't remember feeling that I was better than other kids, just proud of where I came from. My great grandparents were the first white people to live south of Kennan, in what was later to become the Meadow Creek School community. I was proud to be part of a family known for being hard workers, who were honest and tough with strong character. Above all else, we were hunters and woodsmen. My family hunted the big country, where roads were far apart and you needed to be able to find your way and take care of yourself. My great grandmother used to say that if the Edinger men had worked as hard as they hunted, they would have all been millionaires! She also said, with a smile, they had a knack for marrying good women. Both were true. My cousin Dave told me that when he was growing up, sitting on her lap, she would tell him, "You come from good stock. You don't have to take a backseat to anyone!" Somehow my pride overlooked the drunkenness. Very common in families in northern Wisconsin, I think it was extra strong in mine. The rowdiness went with it, although being willing to back things up with your fists wasn't all bad.

The Edinger genealogy is fairly well documented, thanks to my great grandfather's sister, Aunt Bertha. My roots include a passenger on the Mayflower, a Colonel in the Revolutionary War and a soldier for the North in the Civil War. Four great-grandfathers ago is an interesting story about how Charles Moffitt was kidnaped by the Indians of Ohio when he was about ten years old and kept until he was twenty-one.

Following is the Edinger branch of my family as Aunt Bertha wrote it down. It starts in the last half of the 1700's, because Boyd was born about 1790:

The father of William and Boyd Edinger was a large landowner in South Carolina. He became ill and turned the property over to a man who was to use it and in return, care for the boys until they were of age. He was indifferent in caring for them, so they left, changing their name from Edington or Addington. They migrated to Ohio, where both were married, Boyd being the head of this branch of the family. Father (William Washington Edinger) was nine months old when Boyd Edinger (his father) went to Charleston, South Carolina, to settle the estate, in company with his brother William. Boyd contacted Yellow Fever and died. William was never heard from, though many years later, after father was farming and was having his grain stack stenciled, a man showed him an order from a William Edinger, living in Kentucky. They apparently never tried to contact him.

Boyd Edinger was the grandfather to my great-grandfather, Jesse King Edinger. Jesse married Great-Grandma, Gertrude Hart, in 1888. They were living in western Iowa at this time. My grandpa, Clifford, was born in 1891, the second of six surviving children.

I remember two stories Grandpa told of growing up near Kingsley, just east and a little north of Sioux City, Iowa. He said that on quiet, hot, humid summer nights he would go with his mother out to the cornfield, and they could actually hear the corn growing, a kind of rustling, crackling sound. Another time he announced to his mother that he was running away from home. She said, "Alright, go out to the field and tell your Pa." Which he did. His Pa gave him a good spanking and sent him back to the house!

My grandpa was just twelve years old when they came to Kennan, Wisconsin, in 1903. They had bought the land, sight unseen, in April, and made the trip from Kingsley, Iowa, by covered wagon. According to the stories handed down, the trip took almost two months. Great-Grandma packed the clothes they would need for the trip under the mattresses in the back of the wagon. A small wood stove rode under the wagon seat, which was used for cooking. Great-Grandpa set up a tent every night to sleep in. Because there were no maps, they found their way by signs and by asking locals for directions. People along the way were very kind and the young family was often invited to camp in yards and orchards for the night and given fresh milk, butter, vegetables – whatever people could share.

Following a rough trail from Hawkins, the first family they met in Kennan were the Lebals, who had come from the Green Bay area a few years earlier and had settled west of town. Great-Grandpa said he was looking for Section 16, to which Mr. Lebal responded that it was just kitty-corner to where they were at the time. He offered to take the newcomers over to the site in the morning.

While they were unhitching the team, the travelers mentioned a river. Mr. Lebal became suspicious so asked to see their papers. Sure enough, they were looking for Section 16 in the next township to the south. He told my great-grandparents that was wild, totally unsettled country down there and they should find a man in Kennan, named O.B. Green, who knew that country pretty well. So they continued on, camping their first night in Kennan at the first curve of the road, just west of town.

Mr. Green agreed to help Jesse find his property, so a few days later they set out on foot. They followed what our family called "the old tote road." There was a spur line off the main railroad tracks west of town and from there the tote road began, heading southeast, crossing Green, Web, and Meadow Creeks and then crossing the North Fork of the Jump River due east of where Meadow Creek School was later built. From there it followed along the south side of the river, which flowed to the southwest.

The first Edinger spent his first night in the wilds of the Jump River sleeping under a big washed-out pine stump on the south side of the river, just upstream from where County N now crosses the North Fork (locally known as the Black Bridge). As he lay on his bedroll, watching the coals from the campfire die down, I wonder what he felt that night. Was he excited by the country he saw and the challenges he certainly knew were ahead, or was he thinking, "My God, what have I gotten my family into!"

My Great-Grandpa Edinger, Jesse King Edinger. Born June 4, 1864, died July 5, 1936. Married August 23, 1888 to Gertrude Hart.

The next morning they set out again, and after traveling another mile came to the end of the tote road and to the property. There was an abandoned white pine logging camp there. The cook shack had only been covered with tarpaper and not of much use,

13

but the stable and adjoining blacksmith shop was built of sound and sturdy logs. The blacksmith shop would be converted to their living quarters until a new house could be built.

Because it was so far from town, my great grandparents ended up renting places in town for the next few years, so the kids would be able to go to school. A letter has survived, written in 1906, from Great Grandma Gertrude to her father, David Hart, out in South Dakota. By the tone of the letter, I assume he had already visited them in Kennan. She wrote on that October 7th day that they were alone because Jesse was down to the place (the land on the river) with the storekeeper, Mr. Reichert. She tells about how Great-Grandpa was working in the woods for fifty dollars a month plus board for himself and one horse. They are "living in the old hotel with six good rooms and water right at the back door and plenty of barn room with hay costing $3 a month." She is selling milk from a cow they have and relates that butter is 20 cents a pound, 22 cents for a dozen eggs and 40 cents for a bushel of potatoes. At the end, she asks for news of her family and you can tell by the tone of the letter that she sounds very lonely.

There was still a small group of Indians in the area. According to Grandpa Clifford, there was a reservation south of here along the Yellow River. Actually, according to research done by others, and shared with me by Judy Gumz of Westboro, the band were actually squatters. They were affiliated with the band of Potawatami who had been moved from Wisconsin, first to Council Bluffs, Iowa, and then to a reservation on the Kaw River in Kansas after the tribe had ceded their land to the US Government in the 1833 Treaty of Chicago. Beginning in the 1860's, large numbers of these people began migrating back to Wisconsin, to lead a more traditional life. They roved over and lived on unsettled and cutover areas, subsisting off the land. There was intermarrying with neighboring Indian peoples, including the Chippewa. In 1896-97, a large band of these Indians took up residence on the North Fork of the Yellow River, which became known locally as the Indian Farms. It was an ideal location, being fairly remote from White settlements with a major trail of western Taylor County running through there. The site had been used for the grazing of logging company livestock. Oral history places the number of people living at the Farms at approximately 130. In 1900-1901, sixty to eighty of this band died in a horrible smallpox epidemic.

Anyway, Grandpa said every spring the Indians would follow a trail

14

from the Yellow River to the north along the Steve's Creek hogsback (glacial esker) to the Falls on the South Fork of the Jump, where they certainly fished during the spring run. From there the trail ran along the river, down below the Forks, to a place we called the Claybanks. They would spend their summers there. That too was the site of an old logging camp, Grandpa saying those cuts in the high bank were made as spillways to roll the logs in.

The Edingers did visit back and forth with the Indians in the summer. They would have been their nearest neighbors. Grandpa said the chief's name was John Young, and he had long black hair and always had a feather in it. He said, "They used the bark of rock elm to shingle their roofs, which killed the trees. Some angry lumbermen from down below finally run them out," making them stay on the Yellow River. According to the Town of Westboro centennial book, they were finally forced off the Indian Farm and moved to Oklahoma.

Even for the Indians this was hard country. With the heavy stands of white pine just a few years earlier, there had not been much in the way of game. Now that game was beginning to flourish, because of the cut-over land, it was also beginning to attract white settlers. The false ads had told that this cheap land was a place where clover grew wild and farmers could grow tobacco and wheat. The new settlers soon found that the stumps, rocks, and short growing season was going to make farming a subsistence lifestyle at best. Those who still had a little money left over, after trying to make a go of it here, got out. Others like Jesse and Gertrude had to stay. The next seventy years for the Edingers was going to be a hard existence. If it didn't kill them, it would only make them tougher!

LIFE IN KENNAN

The first time my Grandpa Clifford saw Grandma was when she happened to be looking out of the upstairs window of a boarding house in Kennan. Grace Scott had come down to Kennan from Sanborn, near Ashland, Wisconsin, to work with her cousin and her husband as cooks in a logging camp. He thought, "She sure looks pretty," and waved. When she waved back he said to himself, "I'm going to marry that girl." And that's how it turned out.

They had five children; Audrey, my dad Jess, Viola, Clifford, and Donald. When young Clifford was just twelve years old, he was hit by a zinging hockey puck, just below the knee, which broke the skin. He didn't say anything about it until a few days later, when he had an angry red streak running up his swollen leg. Blood poisoning! He died two weeks later in the Ladysmith Hospital with the additional complication of pneumonia.

Times remained tough. There was little hard money to be had, even for someone industrious like Grandpa. They raised, shot, and canned all of their food. The little money that they had was spent on salt, sugar, flour, yeast, tobacco and coffee. Clothes were handmade and what wasn't made was sent for from a catalog.

Grandma Grace and Grandpa Clifford Edinger with Audrey, my dad Jess and Viola in front of their tarpaper shack

There is a photo of the young family when they lived just down the river, which they later lost to taxes. It is of three of the kids in front of Grandpa and Grandma standing in the doorway of their meager home. Literally a shack, with 2x4 studs wrapped with tarpaper. What a desolate looking bunch! I can recall a story my dad told while living down there. He remembered an extra cold winter evening and hearing sleigh bells coming down the river, then swinging off the ice, and coming right up to the door. When he opened the door, the lamplight flowed onto the faces of the team of workhorses, whiskers all white and their breath puffing out the sides of their nostrils. Into the light strode his grandpa, Jesse King, with his broad brimmed hat and heavily frosted mustache.

Grandpa and Grandma Edinger – Clifford and Grace Edinger, about 1953.

In the meantime, my mom was having her own rough life. She was born and raised east of Phillips, out on Emery-Hackett Road. Albina France was a third generation American, her grandparents having come over from the Czech-Slovak region of Europe. My mom's real mom died when she was only two, so she and her older brother, Charlie, lived with their Grandma France for quite a few years, even after Grandpa France remarried. Things did not go well between the two kids and their new stepmother. I remember Uncle Charlie tearing up when he told of their youth and how he tried to make life easier for his little sister. I would characterize my mom as a careful, thoughtful person, certainly not bubbly or spontaneous. She was quiet and preferred to stay in the background but always observant, taking everything in. These traits were probably developed from her childhood as survival mechanisms. She knew how to cope, how to adapt, how to survive. These traits would serve her well in her adult life.

She attended the eight elementary grades at tiny Whitman School. In order to continue her education through high school and then two years at the Normal School in Phillips, she had to stay in town and worked cleaning houses to earn her room and board. On June 9, 1939, she

My Mom, Albina France Edinger, in 1941.

received her diploma from Price County Normal School "having given satisfactory evidence of fitness and ability to teach a Public School." Her first teaching job was that fall at Meadow Creek School. It wasn't long before my dad started courting the new girl in the neighborhood.

They were married early in 1941. Her second year of teaching was her last, because babies started coming along on a regular basis. Larry was the first, followed in fairly regular order by Betty, Nancy, Carol, and Kay. Then there was a four-year break before my year came along, 1951.

Two Edingers were added to the clan in 1951. On March 13, my cousin Lance was born, the last of eleven children. His father, Uncle Dave, and my grandfather were brothers. He chose a most dramatic day to be born. It was in the middle of a horrible spring blizzard and one of their older boys, Forrest, ran up the river to our house to get help. They had no phone at that time. My great-grandmother, who lived just kitty-corner across the field from us, and my grandma, who lived just up the road, and my mom, went down to help with the delivery. Three months later, on June 5, I was born in the Ladysmith Hospital. Someone had to round up my dad, who was pitching at a baseball game that day. I always knew how fortunate I was to have a pal, the same age, to grow up with. We naturally had the same interests – hunting, fishing and trapping. Our adventures together helped shape our adult lives, and we sure had some adventures together. Huck Finn and Tom Sawyer had nothing on us!

Two years after I was born Peggy came along and two years after that Jerry was born. Five girls and three boys. The kids nearly out numbered the cows on our little 80-acre dairy farm. To say our little house was overflowing was an understatement.

My folks had bought the old homestead from Great-Grandma, and Larry and Betty had been born in the old house. But the river had flooded once too many times, so my dad bought the forty just east of their land, most of which was cleared farmland. It was also on the main county road, which had been built in the mid 20's. He added two bedrooms and a kitchen onto the one-room house that was already there, plus a big garage, horse barn and a little dairy barn.

The big garage had been built to house the milk trucks. My dad had started his own business hauling cans of milk from local farmers to the cheese factory. Things had been going pretty well for my folks and it looked like the hard times would finally be over. But then my dad started drinking and fooling around, and it all went to hell. By the time Carol

18

and Kay were born, he had quit drinking for a while but the damage to the marriage was done and they just never got it going in the right direction again.

Growing up, I knew we were poor. We heated the house with wood stoves and never did have running water. We all drank from the same dipper from the water bucket. On especially cold winter mornings, the water would be frozen in the drinking bucket and all of us kids would hustle from our beds to the wood heater and get dressed next to the stove. There was not one stitch of insulation in that house. Heavy blankets and even old coats laid on top, would keep us warm at night and I learned to use my breath to help stay warm by keeping my head under the covers. The roof leaked like a sieve during the summer rainstorms. It became a game for me to put the pots and pans out before the drips began, trying to set them in just the right place. They would try to patch the roof but finding the leaks was not easy. Obviously a re-shingle job was too expensive.

My Dad, his favorite hound, Sox, and a big coyote, about 1943.

Our healthcare was pretty poor, almost nonexistent. You had to be in awfully bad shape before they would cart you off to a doctor or dentist. I remember the terrible toothaches and my mom sitting up with me all night holding me. Crushed aspirin, packed into a cavity would deaden the pain for a while and Mom sometimes would put cloves on the gum next to the toothache. I'm not sure that it relieved the pain but I know it tasted so bad that it made you forget it! Most of the time, we just had to tough it out and let things heal naturally.

One day in the late 50's the Sheriff, Paul Gehring, came knocking on the door. I didn't quite understand what was going on. My dad was crying some, but Mom was her normal stoic self. At one point the Sheriff suggested that maybe we could sell a cow or two. Daddy said no, we needed all the money from the milk. Later, one of the older kids said they might take our home away. Of course the problem was back taxes.

Fortunately for us, the county never foreclosed. Apparently Mom kept paying what she could every year. Several years later I remember how surprised my folks were when we got a notice in the mail saying the back taxes had been paid in full anonymously. We never did learn who we owed such a debt of gratitude to.

Right around the time I started school, my dad started drinking again. As far as the family was concerned he wasn't a mean drunk, but certainly the money was desperately needed elsewhere. I hated alcohol for what it did to him and later what I saw it do to others. Later in our high school years, Lance and I would camp along the river on some Saturday nights. We would have such a grand time! Monday mornings, on the hour and a half ride to school on the bus, our friends would tell about all the fun they'd had over the weekend. Too often it involved drinking parties and their stories would always go something like this. "Boy, did we have fun Saturday night! Bill was passed out by 10:00 and when he came to, threw up all over the back seat. Fred almost fell out of the car when he opened the door to puke and we had to drag him back in by his hair. We were sick all day Sunday. Boy, did we have fun!" Lance and I would look at each other and shake our heads and grin. We knew our definition of fun was better than theirs. To this day I don't drink, have never been drunk, and am proud of it.

I would characterize our family as a traditional family. What we call traditional now was really born out of necessity to survive in a rural, small farm setting. My mom and the kids did the farming because my dad worked out, mostly as a mechanic. He was good at fixing things and could "haywire" anything together. That skill came in handy in such a poor community as ours. I know Mom was disappointed that he would never charge what he was worth.

From the moment a kid was big enough, they had chores. My first chore, in the cold season, was to help my sister Carol bring in firewood every night. When I got older, I had to get hay down out of the haymow and feed cows and either take them to the river for water, almost a half mile away, or pump water for them, with our hand pump, from the well. During the grazing season, I would get the cows in morning and night. When Jerry got older, we would either help each other with these chores or trade off. Everyone was expected to help in the garden in the summer time. I don't remember a lot of whining going on to do the chores. We all realized that we were expected to do our part. Perhaps we gained a sense of importance and self worth, of being needed, from the rest of the family. Being valued by others was a good thing.

We all sat down for supper together at night. Mom had no time for separate meals. We could share our day a little, but our dad didn't tolerate any goofing around at the table. In those days, if someone drove by, it was a big deal and often made suppertime news. "Mrs. Abbrederis went by today," or "Bud and Janet went to town." You had a good idea where they went because of the time it took them to come back. I was a very picky eater. That, plus I was extremely small for my age and skinny as a rail, made a little extra work for Mom. She would make little side dishes for me so I would at least eat something. For instance, she would keep out some noodles before she added the cheese, because I didn't like the two mixed together. The rule was if you put it on your plate, you had to eat it. With all those kids, I don't remember many leftovers, but we always had enough to eat. Ice cream was a real treat, mostly homemade, reserved for birthdays.

Being number six of eight kids, I was raised as much by my older brother and sisters as I was by my parents. Mostly, I was just allowed to be myself, never feeling pressure to be or act a certain way. I had a strong will though. I recall the time I was really small and was trying to set a #1 trap. I was having a hard time getting it set. If I stood on the spring and grabbed the jaws, I could compress the spring using my weight and my arms, but as soon as I tried to spread the jaws, the spring would come back up. About that time my dad came around the corner, "That trap's too big for you, you're going to get your fingers pinched!" Well, I kept at it and after about 10 minutes I finally managed to get it set. I was just admiring my handiwork when my dad came by again. With a pleased look on his face he declared, "Nobody better tell you you can't do something."

Luckily, I was a generally good kid, seldom getting into trouble, not that there is much trouble to get into out in the country. About the worst thing I did was once in the spring, Lance and I started a grass fire between his house and the river so it would green up real nice. We had read that's what the Indians used to do to attract the buffalo and we figured that would work real good for deer too. The fire got going so good that they spotted the smoke from the fire towers and the local fire warden was dispatched. He had no sense of humor, since it had interrupted his evening milking, so Uncle Dave got a fine, which my dad paid half of. We didn't get in much trouble for that, just told not to do it again.

21

Dancing was a big part of our family's entertainment because our dad was the local square dance caller. Auntie Vi told me that Great-Grandpa used to call too, so perhaps our dad wanted to carry on the tradition. Almost all of the local kids belonged to the Rambler's 4-H club and they had dances on a regular basis at the dance hall up on Highway 8 called the Avalon. For music, Miller Floyd played a fiddle and his wife pounded on the piano, as my dad would call, "Alaman left with your left hand, right to your own, now right and left grand." Between square dances were waltzes and polkas, Flying Dutchman, Schottische, Bunny Hop and the Mexican Hat Dance. Luckily the Chicken Dance had not been invented yet, but if it had, my dad would have taught it with gusto!

The center of our community was the one room school up the road; Meadow Creek. It wasn't really one room in that it had a girl's and boy's cloakroom and a small kitchen area. The girl's and boy's toilets flanked the woodshed out back. I loved school, with all those kids to play with during recess, and some learning sandwiched in between. That's how it seemed to me anyway. One teacher for eight grades. Surprisingly, it turned out to be a great system for learning the three R's. Research has shown that kids learn from kids better than adults, so everyone smarter than me was a potential teacher. As long as we were quiet, we could ask for help from any of the other kids. That way, the student teachers were also reinforcing what they had learned.

The school sat on one acre of cleared land, carved out from a corner of the forty-acre school forest. We spent a lot of time in the woods building forts out of grass and brush and logs. In the wintertime, Lance and I set out weasel traps and snares for rabbits. In the spring the ball field got all the attention. Many generations of kids before me had appropriated a corner of Haroldson's cow pasture, and that was our ball diamond. I remember someone would holler, "There's cows in the ball field!" and we would all charge out there and run them off. Playing in fresh cow pies took some of the fun out of the game. We never had real bases, usually a board would do. Sometimes a dry cow pie was pressed into service, but they never held up very well. The rules we played by had a loose resemblance to the official rulebook, not that anyone actually had a real copy. In order to accommodate us little kids, our outs never counted. Winning and losing took a backseat to just playing the game.

The highlight of the school year was, of course, the Christmas program. Some long, low saw horses were placed at one end of the room and then covered with planks for the stage and a wire was strung from wall to wall from which the curtain was hung. Soloists and choirs sang all the traditional songs, wrapped around the main attraction, the play depicting the birth of Jesus. The crowd must have had a hard time keeping all the actors straight since the costumes for the shepherds, wise men, and Joseph were all made from burlap grain sacks! The entire community came, not just parents and grandparents; the place was packed to the rafters. Santa always came in at the end of the program through the back door and distributed gifts.

Although early childhood education and kindergarten were unheard of in those days, for me the Christmas programs started extra early. I loved to sing and if I wasn't singing out loud, at least I had a tune going on in my head. Somehow my older sisters conned the teacher into letting me sing Rudolph when I was four and five. Of course, my family thought I was the star of the show. When I got to the part, "Then one foggy Christmas Eve," I would sing froggy – well, that just added to the cuteness. I remember being scared to death and not looking at the audience but stared over their heads instead, singing to the stovepipe in the back of the room.

For my third and fourth grades, we had a great young teacher named Miss Tews. In preparation for the great event, she would suspend all classes for two weeks. Our music and drama lessons were packed into

All eight grades of the Meadow Creek School at Christmastime in 1959. Front row, from left: My sister, Peggy, then me. Sister Kay is the tallest girl in the back row. The teacher is Miss Tews. I was in the third grade at the time.

those two weeks. At the end of the program, when Santa came in, there was always something about him that reminded me of Miss Tews' boyfriend, Butch. Once my cousin, Rick, got a popgun for a present. A popgun is an air gun that shoots corks. As Santa bent over, next to the tree, to grab another present, Rick shot him right in the butt. We all thought that was hilarious!

Like I said, Miss Tews was a great teacher with a lot of energy, imagination and an overabundance of courage. There was one time we went on a field trip when I was in the fourth grade. Somehow wires got crossed and the bus, which was supposed to bring us back from Phillips, never showed up. Undaunted, Miss Tews packed the entire school, all thirteen of us, into her car . . . a Volkswagen Beetle! Myself and two other little kids crawled into the back window, then the bigger kids sat down and others sat on laps who sat on laps. What a picture that would have made!

On a warm spring day in the fourth grade I can clearly remember Lance and I eating our lunches, on the south side of the school, with our backs against the wall. Lance said, "I heard they're going to close the school." I laughed at the idea and responded, "They can't do that. We have to have a school!" But the rumor was true. They had hatched a plan to add on to the school in Kennan and close all the outlying one-room schools. Industrialized education had invaded my world. You would be hard pressed to find anyone who doesn't have fond memories of attending a one-room country school. The idea behind consolidation was to be able to teach even more, but we lost an awful lot in the bargain.

After Meadow Creek closed, I hated every day of every year of school. It became normal for me to miss ten to twelve days of school every year, most of them spent running my trap line and deer hunting in the fall. We had to take an excuse slip to school explaining our absence, but Mom would never lie. It would always start out with, " Please excuse Gary" followed by "as he was trapping" or "as he was hunting." Somehow I kept my grades up, probably because Mom placed so much importance on it.

All of us kids got different traits from our parents. From my dad I got a sense of how to handle myself out in the woods along with the joy of the hunt. He was a hard worker, but I don't ever remember him pushing anything to the limit. He was more than happy to help any neighbor in need, often times at the expense of his own family. My dad had a plow on the front of his milk truck and during snowstorms in the winter, while picking up milk in the morning, neighbors would give my dad a list of things they needed at Bader's General Store. He would drop the lists off on the way to the milk factory and then pick up and deliver the goods on the way home. He even plowed their driveways at no charge. From him we all learned how to have fun.

Our mom was the one that wanted more for her kids. She worked incredibly hard to try to get it for us. She was the first one up in the morning and the last one to bed at night. Despite being so tired, she always knew if one of us got

My family at Christmas-time in 1958. Back row: Larry, Betty, Carol, Mom and Dad. Middle row: Kay, Me (Gary) and Nancy. Front row: Jerry and Peggy.

up during the night and could even tell who it was by the sounds of our pattering feet on the floor. She was the one that kept the whole thing going, catering to Dad's needs, delegating and overseeing our chores, helping with homework and arbitrating family squabbles, on top of being the main farmer. (All the milking was done by hand.) Mom handled all of the money for the family. Many a time I watched her put bills into three piles; some that absolutely had to be paid, some that she could pay a little on, and some that would just have to wait. We all saw an incredible toughness in her, mentally and physically. She pretty much kept her emotions to herself, never complaining if she was hurting or things were going wrong. Nor was she apt to point out a beautiful sunset or a pretty flower. Once, while she and I were getting firewood in early winter, she showed me what wintergreen was. As she crushed the leaves and sniffed the minty smell, she recalled how her father had shown her when she was a little girl and I could see her drift back to a pleasant memory. I can't ever remember her telling me she loved me; she didn't have to, her actions did and that was enough for me. From her we all got a sense that nothing was too hard, that we could get through it.

Mom went to town once a week to shop at Bader's Store. Saturdays were the big days for shopping for almost everyone, because that's when people had the time to leave their farms. Some places, like Bader's, stayed open until 9:00 on Saturday nights. In my youth, Bader's was as much a public service as it was a commercial enterprise. Besides selling groceries, clothing, hardware, and sporting goods, they even functioned

25

as a bank, cashing checks and extending credit on food and merchandise. When families were having a hard time, Bader's would let them "mark it down" to see them through. We liked it when Charlie, Mr. Bader, waited on Mom. He always threw in an extra bag of candy for us kids.

In the late spring of '67, just before I turned 16, Mom and I were getting some firewood late one morning. As she was dragging a log out to the road, she tripped and fell forward heavily. Instead of getting up, she just lay on the ground, moaning, while holding her stomach and rocking from side to side. I felt so helpless; I didn't know what to do. After about five minutes she got up and said she'd be all right, so we finished getting a load. Over the next few weeks, I caught her holding her stomach in pain many times. She was obviously not all right.

Unknown to anyone except my dad, she had found a lump in her breast many months before. Finally Dad called Nancy in Milwaukee, she was his go to daughter, and told her she needed to come home. There was something wrong with Mom's breast and she would need to talk Mom into letting her look at it.

The cancer was so far along that, at a glance, Nancy knew immediately that it was very serious. For some reason, I went along when Betty and Nancy took Mom to the doctor in Phillips. I remember the date clearly, because it was on my birthday. I waited in the car while they went in. It didn't take very long before Nancy came out crying. After she got in the backseat with me she said, "Oh Gary, he said she only has two years to live!" On the way home, as Betty was driving, she asked, "Why Mom, why? Why did you wait so long?" Her simple answer was, "Some day you will understand."

The doctor got her into the University Hospital in Madison. After running some more tests, they found the cancer had spread to her ovaries and lymph nodes. Mom said she wanted to live until Jerry was out of school, another six years, so they all agreed to go through with some experimental treatments. The cost would be covered by the state. They operated and cut out all the cancer they could and then she had extensive radiation treatments.

With the help of Betty and her husband Tommy, who had their own farm to take care of in Kennan, I became the head farmer. They got me set up with a portable vacuum pump and two milking machines so the chores would be easier. Peggy and Jerry had to step up to the plate too. I don't remember feeling any resentment about the whole situation. Stuff happens. That's just how life is.

26

After the treatments, Mom did get better. She had a whole year of doing really well. I began to hope that the doctor was wrong. But then she started going back to the hospital more and more often and each stay was a little longer. She was now going to the hospital in Marshfield, because that's where her sister, Aunt Aggie, lived. They were very close. Over the years Aunt Aggie had been like a fairy godmother to all of us kids and I'm sure Mom knew Aunt Aggie would do all that she could for our family during her hospitalizations.

The following winter, on our way to check some beaver traps one day, I made some comment about wishing Mom would get better. Larry simply said, "You know, Mom's not going to make it." I remember feeling crushed, but I just nodded. The cancer had spread to her bones and liver.

When Mom became bedridden, my sister, Carol Mae, put her life on hold and came home. We got a hospital bed for Mom and set it up in the living room so she could watch TV and receive company. A lot of very nice people came to visit and help her pass the time. The pain finally got so bad she had to go into the hospital. As if it were yesterday, I can clearly see her struggling to raise herself up off of the stretcher, to wave to us out the back window, as they took her away. I think she knew she would not be coming home again.

My high school graduation was a week later and by then Mom had slipped into a coma. Out in the hallway, after the ceremony, my celebrating was much more subdued than my classmates. Standing there alone, relieved that I would never have to go to school again, I wondered now what? All of the sudden, like you would snap your fingers, two goals became crystal clear. I did not want to be poor, ever again, and I wanted to enjoy life. Were they simple or were they noble goals? I really don't know, but as I write this, forty years later, I feel that I accomplished both.

Mom died June 4, 1969, the day before my eighteenth birthday. She was only forty-nine. Amazingly, or coincidentally, the Phillips doctor's snap assessment had only been one day off. I had been preparing myself for the moment and I had been doing really well until the night of the wake. When it was time to leave, I went up to the casket by myself, and all of the sudden, I just started bawling. As I stood there crying I heard Mom's voice from my right side, like she was standing there right next to me, say, "Don't cry Gary." It was so loud I looked to see if anyone else had heard it, but of course they hadn't. It didn't help. I must have cried for half an hour.

It seems to me that preachers go out of their way to get people to cry at funerals. Perhaps they think that helps in the grieving process. That moment came at Mom's funeral when the minister related, as he had visited Mom, he noticed her looking out the window and asked what she saw out there. When he told of how she saw all her children lined up, the sobbing really got loud in the little Methodist church, but I had gotten it all out the night before. I was behind Dad, as we followed the casket out of the church, when he started wobbling, like he was going to go down. I jumped ahead and grabbed his arm, propping him up. He squeezed my hand so hard it hurt, but once we made it outside he had pulled himself together. We went to the cemetery, where people cried some more. After we left, they put her in the ground, and that was that.

When you read this, you may think that I had a terrible childhood, but I don't feel that way. I had plenty of time to hunt, fish, trap, and play. Having the river nearby added so much more to my life. Every time I stepped out the door, the river was like a magnet, drawing me to her. That's where we all learned to ice skate and swim. It's so easy to remember all of us heading down there to swim after a hot July day of making hay. I can still fee the itchy hay chaff leave my body as I settle into the warm water.

There's another memory about the river that makes me feel warm inside. I'm back in the early 60's. It's late October, before daylight, a crisp, clear morning. As I step out the door I can hear the river calling to the north. The reason I'm out and about so early is to run my trap line. As I reach the edge of the field, I have to turn on the flashlight so I don't get tangled in the fence. As I straighten up, I turn the light off (batteries cost money) and have to wait for my eyes to readjust to the darkness. Closer to the river now, I can make out the individual riffles. Ahead and a little to my right, I can hear the riffles above the pole bridge, so named where the old tote road crossed a little run entering the river there on a bridge made of poles. That's where Grandpa was walking with a character from town one night when a hoot owl let loose nearby. "Whoo, whoo, whoo." The guy responded, "Irish O'Conner from Kennan, who the hell are you?" Quartering to my left I can hear the riffles where we swam. Below that I can just make out the riffles above the Old Swimmin' Hole, where two generations before me learned to swim. Our family calls it the Old Swimmin' Hole but the neighbors call it Grandma's Hole after Great-Grandma Edinger.

28

After feeling my way along a deer trail through the woods, I reached the riverbank. The air above the warmer water is rising and condensing in the cool air and the mist is gently floating upstream. It's that mystical time of first light, when all the night critters have gone to bed and the day critters haven't woke up yet. It's so quiet you can almost hear the mist rise.

When I reach my first set I have to use the flashlight because the water is still dark. By my fourth set, I have some weight in my packsack from a muskrat or two, maybe a rare mink. Between sets, besides wondering what adventure the next set might hold for me, my thoughts wander to things young boys think about; like how to get a kiss from that cute girl at school. The things grownups worry about seem so far away. My thoughts would not have been so carefree had I known my mother would not be there for my high school graduation, that upon graduation I would have to worry about the draft for Vietnam. Forever ended far sooner than I thought it could.

I still get up before daylight on cold October mornings, not for the money I desperately needed back then, but to stay connected to the river and to relive those wonderful memories. We now live in a world that changes far too rapidly. The one thing that remains unchanged is the river. It's something that you can count on, you can lean on and you can escape to. It's always there, intimate and comforting, just like it always has been. I feel so lucky to continue to have the river in my life.

There are so many stories that I could tell. People write entire books about growing up. I could write about the telephone and party lines, where you had to listen to see if someone else was on the line before you dialed, and could listen in on other's private conversations, the impassible roads during spring breakup, neighbors needing to rely on each other to survive, learning to drive when I was 12 with an old pickup truck that had no brakes, driving the tractor pulling the hay baler when I was so small I had to scrunch way down on the seat so I could push the clutch in, the day we tipped over in the school bus, the time my finger got smashed in the pump jack, the traumatic day our family dog, Patsy, died.

Our family is still close, and every time we get together, we reminisce about our shared childhood on our small rural farm. Of all the stories, the two big events that are told and retold are the time our house caught on fire and the day we tipped over in the boat.

FIRE AND WATER

"Come on Gary, get up, the house is on fire!"

It was February of 1956 when our house caught on fire. I was four and a half years old. My mom had just gotten up in the middle of the night to throw more wood in the stoves, as she did every night. As she lay in bed, trying to get back to sleep, she suddenly saw flickering shadows in the dining room. Not even wasting time to investigate, she started screaming, "Fire! Fire!" as she was leaping out of bed.

I was in the other bedroom, just off the kitchen, sleeping with my four older sisters in the big bed, with Larry sleeping on the other side in a single bed. Peggy was in a crib at the foot of Larry's bed and Jerry was in a crib in our parent's bedroom. I remember quite a ruckus, as kids bailed out of the bedroom, but since I didn't know what was going on, and no one grabbed me, I was trying to fall back to sleep. That's when one of my sisters came back and got me. When I entered the kitchen, there was Mom, right in the act of throwing a bucket of water at the angry flames, where the kitchen stove pipe disappeared into the wall. The floor was all wet.

Most of us huddled up next to the entrance door, where I could see into the dining room. Nancy was on the phone, calling neighbors to come and help while Mom told Betty to start carrying clothes out. Larry and Daddy were fighting the flames shooting out next to the dining room stove. I got scared and started crying. That's when Dad whirled around and bellowed, "Get the hell outa here!" So we piled outside and scrambled into the nearest refuge, the car. It was really cold in there. I just had on my long underwear.

On her first trip outside, Betty's wet feet stuck to the frozen porch and peeled off some of the skin. She quickly pulled on some wool socks and kept going, throwing arm-loads of clothes on top of us in the car. It wasn't long before flames began licking out of the gable end of the roof on the far end of the house. Someone came out and tried to get the car started, to move away from the house. It did not want to start, so the girls started praying, "Please God please, please start the car." They'd had a lot of practice doing that; the old junker could be stubborn, even on a warm day. Finally, the engine caught and we backed the car away from the house and parked next to the barn. As we moved from the car into the warmer barn, the neighbors began to arrive. With Mom manning the pump handle and enough people, including Larry and Betty, carrying water, they got the fire out. My cousin Duane slid off the icy roof and landed on his back, but luckily avoided serious injury.

We ended up going to Auntie Vi and Uncle Buster's place to spend the rest of the night. Everyone went in except for me. Like I said, I only had my long underwear on and was too embarrassed. When Auntie Vi came looking for me, she laughed off my silliness and took me by the hand and led me up the steps into her warm home. I had to stay there a few more days while my folks patched up the place good enough to move back in. Because we lived in a hardy, self-reliant community, where men could size up the situation quickly and could spring into action without having to be told what to do, our home was saved. Our home wasn't much, but it was the only one we had. It was so nice to be able to go back home again, charred walls, smoky smells and all.

*   *   *   *   *   *

A year and a half after the house fire the other traumatic family experience occurred. I remember it was in the middle of June because I had just gotten a new pair of tennis shoes for my sixth birthday. The area had been inundated with heavy rains and the river was really rolling, way over its banks, as high as it often gets during spring breakup. My brother Larry and a bunch of other young people had borrowed an old rowboat from a nearby hunting cabin (they weren't using it!) and had been floating the river all day. Larry had fashioned some crude paddles out of one-inch boards because there were no oars. They would throw in a few miles upstream, where the county road bumped the river, and float down to Bud and Janet Edinger's, portaging the road at the Black Bridge because there was only a foot of clearance under the bridge. At Bud and Janet's they wrestled the boat up the bank, threw it on a hayrack, hauled it back upstream and did it all over again.

When my dad got home from work that evening and heard about what had been going on all day, he figured the rest of us kids should get in on the fun too. Our dad knew how to have fun. I begged Mom if I could go along and finally she said, "I suppose, just don't get your new

31

shoes wet." Dad tried real hard to get Mom to go too, but she didn't know how to swim and didn't want any part in it. Besides, there were chores to do.

We would have to make a shorter trip of it because it was getting late, so we put in by the Black Bridge. It just so happened that my cousins were also going to float the river. They had taken a big tractor innertube and laced a plywood floor in it, so they pushed off just ahead of us; I think Duane, David and Forrest were among them. In our boat there was Dad, Larry, Betty, Carol, Kay and I. Nancy didn't go because she didn't like outdoorsy stuff and Peggy and Jerry were too little. There was not a lifejacket in the bunch – you couldn't waste good money on something silly like that! I had never been in a boat before and I was a little afraid as we drifted away from the bridge, but the smooth rolling of the river soon helped settle my nerves.

At the second bend in the river, a fishing hole known as the Pole Bridge, the current swept us into the bank nose first. I was sitting on the back seat and just like that, I was over the front seat and scrambling across the bow, headed for dry ground. "Hey, hey, where you going?" Dad said as he grabbed my leg and hauled me back in.

They pushed away from the bank, but without oars the boat was proving to be unwieldy. About 200 yards downstream we encountered a sweeper. The roots of the old hard maple had been undercut by the current and was leaning out over the river, just above the surface, its branches 'sweeping' the water. My dad realized we were going to be in trouble and I remember him urging Larry, "Paddle, paddle!" trying desperately to get out far enough from the bank so we would clear that tree. But the paddlers were too inept and the surging current proved to be too strong. The bow hit the tree first, then the boat turned broadside to the current and over we went. I forgot to mention that I didn't know how to swim.

Somehow I hit the water right side up, so I torpedoed straight down, well below the surface. The water was really dirty and all I saw as I was going down were bunches of air bubbles rising around me. I should have been scared but oddly I felt real calm and everything seemed to go into slow motion. Right about the time I stopped sinking, I began to dog paddle, as much by instinct as anything else. It worked and I was rising rapidly when "Bang!" I hit my head on something hard. It drove me back down, so I started paddling again and "bang" I hit my head a second time. It turned out I was drifting right underneath the overturned

32

boat. I didn't sink very far the second time, so on my third try I stuck my hand up, so I wouldn't hit my head again.

As luck would have it, my hand came up alongside the outside of the boat, right next to where my ten-year-old sister Kay was hanging onto the side of the overturned craft. The way she tells it, as she was drifting along with the boat, a skinny little hand came popping out of the water right next to her. So, she reached over and grabbed it and ploop, up popped Gary!

As soon as I broke the surface, the fear I had been repressing came boiling out. "Heeelp!" I hollered. Kay tried to calm me with "Sshh, sshh. It's all right. Get up on the boat." I put my arm up on top, but I couldn't pull myself up. There was no keel to grab onto.

In the meantime, my dad was having a heck of a time. He was naturally afraid for me, since I was the littlest, and so the first thing he did was start reaching around in the murky water, trying to find me. He got a hold of a skinny wrist and pulled it in. It turned out to be Carol Mae. Betty, too, was trying to find someone to save and had a hold of Carol from the other side. When Dad pulled her away from Betty, Carol reacted like a lot of drowning victims do by clamping onto his back and wrapping her arms around his neck. He was a good swimmer so he headed for the surface. At one point Carol remembers Daddy had his hand over her face, perhaps trying to keep her from swallowing water. Just like me, he kept coming up under the boat. He knew if he didn't get air on his third try, it was going to be their last and they were both going to drown. He reached up with his hand, found the side of the boat, and pushed it out of the way. He managed to suck in enough air to get enough strength to peel Carol's arms off from around his neck.

Right where we were, the river channel made a slight bend to the northwest, but because the water was so high, the main current went straight ahead, through a sparse grove of river bottom maples. A big driftwood pile had formed in what was now the middle of the river, held there by a clump of maples. He headed for that, with Carol in tow. When Betty came up, she was behind the boat and everyone else. When she spotted Dad and Carol heading downstream toward the driftwood pile, she took after them. It was easy swimming for her, she said, all she had to do was stay on top.

By then, Larry had found Kay and I. He told Kay we'd have to swim to shore so they put me between them and let the boat go. Of course, Kay wasn't that strong of a swimmer, and pretty soon, I was going under. At one point I remember Larry yelling, "Keep his head up, keep his head up!" Kay responded, "I'm trying." She was having a hard enough time just trying to keep herself afloat. I got pretty good at taking a big gulp of air every time my head came up. Later, my dad said he didn't know how a sixteen-year-old kid managed to keep both of us afloat. The last time my head came out of the water, the driftwood pile was right in front of my face. The current had fed all six of us onto the driftwood pile!

My cousins had heard the ruckus and happened to be in shallow water, so they jumped off their raft and spread out, figuring they might have to catch someone. They did catch the boat and brought it back up to us. As we were all huddled together on the driftwood pile, my dad saw I was feeling pretty glum. "What's the matter Gary?" he asked. With a sorrowful, guilt laden voice, I replied, "Mom said not to get my shoes wet." He roared with laughter, gently shook my shoulder and said, "I think she'll be all right with it this time."

Everyone had lost their appetite for a boat ride, but we still had to get to shore so we could walk home. I refused to get in the boat. My dad tried reasoning with me first. "We're just going over there, it'll be all right." "No, I'm not getting in." "Well, what are you going to do?" Me, "Wait till the water goes down." "Well, that will be three days!" Me, "I don't care, I ain't getting in the boat!" He finally gave up, so kicking and screaming, they carried me into the boat and held me down till we reached the shore. From there it was only a fifteen-minute hike back to the house. Mom and Nancy were in the barn milking when we got home.

Mom was so upset with Daddy for putting her kids in such a dangerous situation and so relieved that we were all right, that she began to cry. It was one of the few times I ever saw her cry and I got an extra strong hug from her. Dad was right; she didn't say a word about my wet shoes!

What a miracle that no one had drowned! How many times could you throw a six-year-old kid, who didn't know how to swim, into the middle of a raging river and have it come out all right? Surprisingly, the experience did not make me afraid of water, but I was definitely afraid of boats. It would be another six years before I would set foot in a boat again.

Chapter 5

A HUNTER'S JOURNEY

From the beginning, I was a hunter. My earliest memory of trying to get something was with my toy suction cup arrows and bow. I suppose I was about three at the time. My mom drove the school bus, which was our family car, and hauled the local kids to our one room school and I rode along. We had dropped off the last of the school kids one evening and stopped down to visit Great-Grandma Edinger, who lived just kitty-corner across our forty-acre field. On the way down her little lane, I spotted a critter out in our field and in my small brain figured it had to be a rabbit. As soon as the car door opened, I bolted for the field, grasping my toy bow and arrows declaring I was going to get that rabbit. My mom and older sister probably thought it was cute until they spotted my prey. I remember them hollering to stop and come back, but I was on a mission. The short-eared, black-and white-striped, long-furry-tailed "rabbit" fortunately saw me in plenty of time and headed for the tall weeds. Luckily, I never did catch up with it!

As soon as I was old enough to beg, my dad never got out of the house to go hunting or fishing without me tagging along. My favorite trick, if all else failed, was to stand on the porch, crying, as he was leaving. It always worked. I first started going with him bow hunting in the fall. He was the first archery hunter in this community, using equipment only one model improved on what the Indians had used. The only rule was that I had to be quiet.

He would pack me on his back, taking a blanket along to plop me down on, when we got to the spot for the evening

My dad and his first deer taken with the bow, about 1956.

35

watch. When hunting, he always had a box of Vicks cough drops in his shirt pocket and he would always share one with me. The cigarettes were already getting to him. He used to brag to his friends how I was "quiet as a mouse" while we waited for a deer to walk by. Mostly I remember falling asleep a lot.

While driving home from the visitation, the eve of his funeral in 1988, it was the memory of Vicks cough drops and feeling his strong shoulder muscles rippling under my skinny arms wrapped around his neck that prompted my wife, Leanne, to ask quietly if I wanted her to drive. The road got kind of hard to see there for a little while.

After I was too big to carry, I was expected to keep up. My little legs would burn with the lactic acid buildup within the first quarter-mile, before I would get my second wind. It never seemed to matter how hard the hike was, I was raring to go the next time. I remember, we would be going along, and all of a sudden he would stop, turn around, and ask, "Which way to the house?" or "Which way to the car?" I always tried to pay attention, so my answers were usually right. He would get a pleased grin on his face, say "Yup" and we would continue on.

Because the previous three generations had to hunt in order to survive, it was natural for me to become a hunter. From stories Grandpa told me, it sounded like his dad fell into the subsistence lifestyle pretty easily. One story in particular I remember well. They were down on the hogsback, in early fall, hunting deer with the neighbors. In the beaver pond below, a doe started out across the pond, and everyone else started shooting. After a shot or two, they figured it was too far and stopped wasting expensive ammo. Great-Grandpa asked, "You boys done?" Someone responded, "I guess so Jess," to which Great-Grandpa threw up the long octagon barreled .30-.30, took careful aim, and dropped her.

About thirty-five years ago, I bumped into a very old fellow visiting in town. Upon learning who I was, he related another great story. Years ago, he was down in my neighborhood working for the owner of a threshing machine. They were just finishing up at this place when Great-Grandpa came up the road with a team and a wagon to let them know he had some oats to thresh, they could spend the night with him, but he had no meat. The teller of the story said he and his partner slept in the same bed that night and just before daylight, he heard the screen door open and close. He poked his buddy in the ribs and said, "We're gonna have venison for breakfast." and sure enough they did.

The champion marksman in the family, though, was Grandpa's

brother, Uncle Dave. Grandpa said to me once, "He should have been. He shot everything that moved!" Frosty Adomitas, a Kennan resident, enjoyed sharing the story about this one time, when he was a kid. Frosty had stayed overnight with my cousins Moose and young Dave. He awoke at daylight with someone tugging on his big toe. Uncle Dave had his finger to his lips and then whispered, "Let's go hunting."

As they were slipping along the river that morning, they caught a yearling doe crossing upstream. The rifle butt had barely touched Old Dave's shoulder before it went off. The water flew beyond the deer and Frosty yelped, "You missed!" Old Dave worked the lever action, let the hammer all the way down and then pulled it back on half cock (safety). As the rifle settled in the crook of his arm he responded, "Not by much." By then the yearling had gained the bank and, as if on cue, fell over dead. "Not by much."

It was stories like these and literally dozens of others I drank in as I was growing up. At gatherings, older men would ask me, "You gonna be a buck hunter?" like that was the ultimate. From the suction cup arrows, I graduated to a BB gun and by the age of eight Mom allowed me to use the single shot .22, as long as I was alone. The red squirrels and blackbirds weren't very safe when I was around and in the fall I was really proud to bring a grouse home for supper.

It seemed like the November of my twelfth birthday would never arrive. I was schooled in our family's rules of deer hunting: make the first shot count. Your first shot is your best shot (meaning if you have a good shot take it, don't wait for a better one), hold right behind the shoulder (head and neck shots are too risky) and the animal belongs to the hunter who has first tracking blood, not the one who shoots it last.

For deer Dad gave me the old Model 94 .32 Winchester Special. Grandpa had bought it for him used when my dad was thirteen. Dad had shot his first "hard-horned" buck with it along with many others, which he had documented by filing a notch for each in the metal butt plate. As I counted off the twenty-five notches, he said he had quit filing a long time ago. My older brother had killed his first buck with it and now it was my turn.

We went up to Bader's General Store and Old Charlie sold us a half-a-box of 170-grain silvertips because that's all the budget allowed. I laugh when I think of trying to do that now! The bullet holes in the fifty-yard target were oblong from the old wore out barrel, but Dad said I was good enough to get the job done. That first evening of season found

Standing in front of my first buck.

me putting my own notch in the butt plate. I was a buck hunter!

But deer hunting opened up more than just being able to kill a deer. I already knew and understood tradition. My dad liked the big country, the wild places. At the time, the land had healed from the last round of logging in the '30s and this new area he was showing me was truly trackless. It was, in fact, big enough to get lost in.

That fact was born out by the story of Bill Faulk, who had gotten lost in this same area deer hunting in the early part of December of 1926. Bill was related by marriage, having married Grandma Edinger's sister, Aunt Zol. They were living at the Falls at that time. (It is hard to believe now, but at one time there was a big farm there, Grandpa saying he had pulled the first stumps there with a team of horses.)

That fateful day, Bill had been hunting with the Fenske gang. They were a group of hunters from the New London area who had a tent camp a mile and a half upriver. Evening found them down along Wolf Creek. The brothers invited Bill back to their camp for coffee, but Bill declined, saying it would be far easier to just cut north, cross the river on the ice, and be home in short order. The weather was bitter cold.

Somehow he never found the river and ended up wandering west instead of north. While desperately trying to find his way in the dark, panic overcame him, and he left his gun, throwing off his coat, hat, and mittens as he went. Sometime well after midnight, he wandered onto the Owen Lumber Company railroad grade, over in Rusk County. Following it to the north and west, he crossed the river on the trestle and about a mile further, came to the railroad roundhouse. The fireman stationed there that morning was just firing up the engine when he heard a noise at the door. He found Bill Faulk there, severely frozen. They rushed him to the Ladysmith Hospital with the engine, but Bill died three days later from gangrene.

Although I was well aware of this story growing up, I never felt the woods was a dangerous place. On the contrary, that's where I felt the most confident and safe. I didn't like going to the bigger towns, where there was the hustle and bustle. I never went through a door first, if I could help it and once inside, wanted to be in a corner with my back to the wall. I'm still that way. For me, the woods is my church, a place that is safe and familiar. There is nothing you can't handle in nature, as long as you keep your head. I learned that from my dad. It was a lesson that would later save my life more than once.

Like my dad, I also inherited the knack for finding my way in the woods. Already during my first year, he recognized that by asking me to take the older hunters around on some of our deer drives. Being entrusted by that kind of responsibility helped fuel my Edinger pride. Without my realizing it, Dad had put me on the path of addiction for wild places.

I fell in love with those deep woods. It seemed like the farther I got from the house or vehicle, the more it felt like I was really hunting. Having that feeling of really hunting became just as important as getting something. Only once, while I was still in high school, was I put to the test of being lost, being forced to keep my wits. It was during deer season and just when it was time to leave my stand that evening, I heard a deer coming. I was sure it was a buck, because of the deep grunting sound he was making. By the time he came through, I could barely make out his body, let alone see the sights.

After the deer was gone, it was fairly dark, but I wasn't worried. Although it was a good mile out of there, my landmarks were pretty easy to follow on the way out. After crossing two natural openings in the woods, I had a big spruce tree to go to and then a big white pine, before crossing a little willow draw and then climbing a ridge. From the ridge I would be able to hear the river.

When I reached the big old white pine, for some reason I stopped to look up into its dark top. When I started out again, my sense of direction was off, so instead of going northwest, I ended up going due west. I stumbled through the brush for a long time, suppressing a pretty good dose of anxiety, before finally being forced to admit that I was turned around. When I spotted the dark top of a spruce tree against the night sky up ahead, I headed for that, planning to use its dead lower branches to start a fire (I had matches) and wait for Dad to come and find me. When I struck a match, I saw some twine hanging down through the spruce's branches, and instantly recognized it as another one of our deer stands. I put the match out, and as the skyline came into focus, my head spun like a compass inside and click, just like that, my true sense of direction was back. I easily walked the one-half mile out to the river and met Dad coming to find me on the drive home.

Although I can't remember anyone really voicing them, a self-imposed, higher set of standards applied to deer hunting during legal season. (Despite the DNR laws, our family season was from the Fourth of July to New Year's Day.) The big bucks were worthy of respect and in order to feel like you had done something good and honorable, the chase had to be fair. There was nothing fair about shooting over a salt lick or with a light. Except for shooting straight, the other hunting skills were not needed. If you wanted to feel good about your buck, you had to earn it and that included time spent scouting to the long hard drags out of the woods and everything in between. This buck hunting was a heck of a lot more than just making meat.

My favorite story of hunting with my dad came along when I was about sixteen. There was tracking snow on the ground, as he was taking the guys around to stand off the next drive, and they jumped a nice buck in some open black ash. The buck headed into the wind, as they often do, and in that direction lay a big horseshoe bend in the river, about a mile away. Dad figured the buck would probably stop and lay down, rather than cross the river in the daylight. After we finished the drive, he told Larry to take everyone and try to get around that buck by standing it off along the river, making sure to close off the sides. My dad and I would track him through.

Once we got on the track, he had me stay off to his left a little and "watch like a hawk ahead." He stayed on the track. The buck's track continued on into the wind and finally we were near the river. The flat was thick with hazel and gooseberry brush and before we started into it, he quietly said over to me, "Get ready. If he laid down, he's gonna be in here." We hadn't gone another fifty yards when, out of a patch of gooseberry brush not more than eight paces ahead, the buck leaped into flight, quartering away to our left. He had lain tight as long as he could, having smelled and heard Larry station guys ahead and then, when we came up from behind, he knew that he was trapped. As the .32 Special was flying to my shoulder, I hauled the hammer back and as soon as the butt plate snugged into my shoulder, I pulled the trigger. The deer took one more jump before my dad's .308 went off and down he went. My eyes were glued to the spot where he went down, waiting to make sure he didn't get up again, when I heard my dad say, "You were quicker, but I was straighter!" and then a little chuckle. The saying "A cool eye and a steady nerve beats simple quickness every time" was once again proven to be true.

After my first year of hunting under my dad's wing, I started tagging along with Larry more. I liked going with him because he hunted harder. At the very end of my second season, I still hadn't filled my tag. There was still about forty-five minutes of daylight left, but Dad and the rest of the crew were calling it quits. Larry really wanted me to get a buck, plus he just really liked to hunt, so he sent me up to the bend of the river above the Black Bridge, as he pushed out that little flat on the north side. Although nothing came out, that was the beginning of a long tradition between us to hunt to the very end of every season. Only once since then did the entire crew fill up. We couldn't hunt the last day, because no one had an open tag and we both thought that really stunk. We just hated to quit.

Sometime during my high school years, I was out one morning hunting for grouse. I stepped into this little opening when all of a sudden crows were jumping in the air in front of me. In no time, the old 12 gauge went off four times and I had three dead crows. As I picked up the last one, I remember this feeling of uneasiness inside. Holding the three birds in front of me, I began to wonder, what was the point? I'd wasted four good shells for what; three dead things I couldn't use and really hadn't been hurting anything. That was when I began to question the way I did things and how my actions impacted others. My changing ethics was a long, slow process. Sometimes a certain thing happened, like with the crows, and the process was quickened, but generally I would describe it as an evolution. Like I tried to show earlier, I came from a long line of people who had to hunt and gather from the land to survive. Because of the scarcity of money, almost all rural families in northern Wisconsin had ignored the fish and game laws of the state. My family was one of the last to get the message that fish and game belonged to the state and was not free for the taking, any time you wanted to. From the point of view from those before me, nobody had the right to tell them they couldn't feed their family. In the course of "violating', as it was called around here, Wisconsin Conservation Wardens were regarded as mere pests, although my relatives did everything they could not to get "pinched". There certainly was no money in the budget to be paying fines.

41

The only time, that I know of, that Grandpa Clifford got caught was the time Grandma sold a buck to undercover wardens. They owned and were living on the land down at the Forks at the time and Grandpa had shot a very nice buck legally. (It was skinny as a rail but had a nice rack.) Grandpa was gone, when the wardens came knocking, and the $50 they were offering (a lot of money in those days) sure looked better than that tough old buck! Grandma figured Grandpa could shoot a nice fat doe anytime.

I think by the time my dad's generation came of age, there was the added element of having some excitement in their life. Many of the young men had returned from WWII and Korea and life was pretty boring in a town like Kennan, after what they had experienced. They probably would have been okay had they continued hunting off the back forty, but with cars and spotlights and shooting deer off others people's fields, the danger of getting caught increased tenfold. My cousin Dave, who lost an eye in Korea, practically

Grandpa Edinger, my dad and his brother, Uncle Don, about 1937. My Dad is holding his old .32 Special.

became a legend in these parts when it came to outwitting wardens. When Dave taunted the warden one night by telling him he would never catch him, the game was on.

The best story Dave tells of eluding the wardens was the night his brother Forrest was doing the driving, helping him get a piece of meat. Right after the shot, headlights and flashing red lights suddenly sprang to life behind them and the chase over the dusty, backcountry roads was on. They headed east and crossed the ford of the river at the place we called Haroldson's corner, hoping the wardens wouldn't drive across the slightly swollen river too. The warden's car was more tenacious than that, so the chase continued on towards County I. Just before they got to County I, there was a real sharp hill to fly over. Dave told Forrest to slam on the brakes as soon as they were over the hill and he would jump with the gun. The car was still going 30 MPH when Dave bailed out, so he hit the gravel hard, as Forrest drove on. The impact jarred the gun loose from his grasp. The only reason he was able to hang onto it was that the front sight got caught in the web of skin between his thumb and forefinger. Sliding down the road he started rolling for the ditch, hoping not to get run over by the trailing warden's car in the swirling dust. Except for having to pick a lot of gravel out of his hide, he had to pay no other penalty that night.

He finally did get caught. Dave was driving that night while his brother-in-law, Red Purdum, did the shooting. Same as before, the warden's car had been following with their lights off. Once again the chase was on, only this time they headed west, onto Green Creek Road. Dave told Red to throw the gun into the water, as they flew over Web Creek. At the first corner, Dave was going too fast and the car ended up out in the weeds. The wardens were at the doors in an instant, the chief warden claiming with glee, "We got you now; we got you now! We saw you throw the gun." The violators got hauled back to Web Creek and when the spotlight was played onto the weeds, next to the creek, there was the rifle, stuck in the mud barrel first. Red had missed the creek by 20 yards! The stock stuck up there so plainly, it might as well had a flag tied on it! That was the end of Dave's perfect record.

Just after I was born, the state figured it was time to get control of this large family group. The Edingers had been living off the land long enough. That early fall morning, all six Edinger households south of Kennan woke up with two warden cars parked in their yard. It was like a regular FBI raid. At our house, they had already searched the outbuildings and found nothing. They wanted to search the house, but Dad told them no, not without a search warrant. Of course, we had illegal meat in the freezer. While one warden car had to go the thirty miles to Phillips, to get the judge to sign a search warrant, the other car sat in the yard, keeping an eye on the place. My folks hatched a daring plan to smuggle the meat out of the house. The cows had to be milked yet that morning and the milk house was right next to the house, so every time Mom dumped a pail of milk into the milk cans, she would come into the house. They would put some packages of venison in the

43

bottom of the milk pail, which she carried right past the warden's car, back to the barn. The house was empty by the time they searched it.

Poor Mom. She must have been so scared. To pay a fine would have been really hard on the family. Like I said before, she was really tough and willing to do anything to survive. I'm sure after it was over she leaned on Dad pretty hard to quit his violating ways. He needed more persuading than that. He had to get pinched three times before he finally got the message.

The last time was when the warden claimed he saw Jess Edinger run on top of water. Dad had lost the privilege to buy a hunting license the year before, so that year he bought one in my mom's name, so he could hunt during legal deer season. At least he would have the required back tag, he would kill a buck, and Mom would register it. Sounded like a good plan.

That evening he ended up by the Black Bridge, just a half-mile north of the house. Trying to be cautious, he figured he'd cross in the riffles, just below the bridge, rather than expose himself on the road. Because the riffles were making too much noise and perhaps the wind was wrong, he didn't hear the car coming until it was almost at the bridge. He took off running. Of all the luck, wouldn't you know it, it was the wardens. A man running across the river looked mighty suspicious, so somehow they rounded him up. When they asked him for his name, he gave them my mom's name, Albina, a very unique name and he hoped clearly not as feminine as Mary or Sue. So they asked for some other ID and Dad said he'd left his wallet at the house. "Well, let's go to your house."

Dad played it out right to the door. As he was opening the door, he turned and said, "All right, the jig is up, you got me." One of the wardens slid past my dad into the kitchen, where he could see my mom standing and said, "Hi Albina." She said, "Hi Frank." They had gone to high school together! As they were leaving, he kidded my dad by saying it was the first time he had ever seen a man run on top of the water.

Sometime in the early '80's I was racing sled dogs over near Green Bay. I had done well the first day, so my name was in the paper there. After Sunday's run, as I was putting the dogs away, an old man came up to me and asked if I was related to a Jesse Edinger over there in Price County. When I told him he was my dad, he proceeded to share the story about the time he was a game warden and had witnessed a man run on water. I laughed and told him he didn't have to finish the story, I had heard it many times. He said it was one time he didn't feel good about

44

writing out a ticket. It was obvious how poor we were. Another fine was clearly going to be a hardship on our family. Had he been alone, he said, he would have turned and walked away. I thought that was really something, that he had taken the time to look me up. My family had obviously left an impression on him.

I got in trouble with the wardens only once. Right after I graduated from high school, I was down on the flowage trapping muskrats that fall. It was the first year the state changed from requiring you buy a trap tag from them for every trap to just attaching your own metal name tag. Since I didn't know where to get name tags, I didn't bother. Besides, I'd never run into a warden while trapping anyway.

So, I was checking my traps with the canoe and by pure accident, caught a small beaver. I'd had beavers accidentally get caught before, but they were so strong that they had always pulled free from the small muskrat traps. This one had gone out to the end of the drowning stake and drowned. The problem was that beaver season didn't open for two months yet. In a situation like this, you are supposed to leave the non-target animal in the trap, call the DNR, and take them back, where they would remove the animal from your trap. That was going to be too much bother, besides, I didn't have name tags on my traps, so I decided to take it home and skin it. I sure couldn't throw it in the brush and waste it.

Right when I got back to the landing, here came the warden and his helper. At first I thought it was perfect timing for them, but probably they had me staked out. They grabbed the illegal beaver and made me pick up all my traps, about twenty of them, which they confiscated along with the thirteen muskrats I'd caught that day, because of the lack of name tags. The chief warden left me with a $29 fine for no name tags and an $80 fine for trapping beaver in closed season.

When I got home, Dad said I should fight the beaver charge. If I lost, he'd pay the court costs. I posted bond on the $29 fine because I was guilty. When my court date arrived, I went up to Phillips to face the judge. I just told the story as I have already lain out but added that if I had been trapping beaver, I would have set a #4 trap not a #1. (The higher the number, the larger the trap.) I wouldn't be trapping beaver now anyway, because they weren't prime yet. That little beaver wasn't hardly worth skinning, but that is what I intended to do and get what I could for it because I couldn't waste it.

As I sat back down, the judge began to render his verdict. Judge Bjork had quite a reputation for being a fair man and he was true to his colors that day. He began, "I understand your predicament, young man, so my decision is to find you guilty on the count of no name tags. On the count of trapping beaver in closed season, I find you morally innocent, but legally I must find you guilty. Therefore, I fine you $29 on both counts and order the DNR to return your traps and all your muskrats."

At that the warden jumped to his feet and began to protest. "But your honor, we have already skinned the 'rats and besides…" The judge rather angrily cut him off. "I know the difference between a #4 and a #1 trap! This young man was not trapping beaver and trapping is an important part of his economy! Don't bring another case like this in here!" You can imagine how wide my grin was as I thanked the judge.

After we stepped out into the hall, the warden stopped and turned to his helper and said, "See, I told you." Then he turned to me and explained, "On the way in here today I told him, 'You watch; when these Edingers take the stand, they always tell the truth'." There was a hint of respect in his voice, but before I could get my chest puffed out too far, he came back with, "But if I ever catch you again, I'm going to throw the book at you!"

I followed him to his house, where he returned my traps and all the muskrats, already skinned and stretched. I sure came out of that smelling like a rose!

For us and many of our neighbors, life was a constant cat and mouse with the Wisconsin Conservation Wardens. I think people accepted that wardens had their job to do. It was also generally accepted that if you got caught, you took your medicine because people accepted responsibility for their actions. Living off the land was a necessity for many. It was hard for them to think long term when they were just trying to get through today. They would deal with tomorrow when it came. I'm not trying to make excuses, that's just how it was.

Over the course of many years, my views on fish and game laws have changed. Currently, I go out of my way to follow them and it's not from the fear of getting caught as much as feeling it's the right thing to do! I used to think game laws were there to make it harder to get something. Now I understand they're there to ensure the survival of the species, in fairness to other hunters, and to make sure our advances in technology don't overwhelm the animal's gifts to escape, to keep it hunting and not killing. What I don't understand is why I changed when others, who grew up like me, still cling to the old adage, "Laws are meant to be broken." I wish I knew why I changed. I wish I could explain it. I can't. I know preaching doesn't work. Like so many other things in this world, laws and rules go only so far. When there is no one at hand to temper our actions, we all revert back to what is right for ourselves at that moment. It all comes down to what is inside you.

There has been another evolution going on alongside my changing ethics. It's the reasons why I hunt. The tradition of hunting still burns strong inside of me. The need to get something is much lower on the list now than it used to be. I think I hunt for every reason that's ever been expressed. I hunt for the meat. If I don't like to eat it, I don't shoot it. I also hunt for a trophy. I hunt to hone and practice my marksmanship and woodsmanship skills, to test myself against nature, to be a part of nature, for the comradeship of a select few, to have time alone. The quality of the hunt is diminished if any one of these elements is lacking. I also hunt now to pass it on. My son, Garret, is turning into a pretty good hunter. He has added his own notch next to his grandfather's and mine on the butt plate of the Old 32. I find myself judging him on how he hunts rather than if he gets something. I think he understands the why, the same as I did with my dad. It looks like my family's hunting link into the future is in good hands.

I'm well aware of those who would take issue with the idea of killing animals as a noble tradition. As I have been trying to explain, for many of us, killing is a small reason of why we hunt, but in the end we do "kill in order to have hunted" as the Spanish philosopher Gasset has said. At least I can argue back that procuring your meat from a self-sustaining ecosystem is far less objectionable than the commercial means by which our food is supplied to the market.

Hunting is a very real activity where, if you choose, you can immerse yourself in the laboratory of the real world and escape from the insulated one we have built around ourselves. I do not like the term "sport," when it comes to hunting. I left that part far behind with my youth, much the same as a kitten, as it matures, quits pouncing on butterflies. Once you witness the light fade from an animal's eye, you cannot escape the commonality we have with animals. Someday the light, too, will fade from our eyes and once you make that connection, that final reality is very sobering. It forces you to comprehend what death really is and there is nothing sporting about that.

Hunting differs from sports in other ways too. You don't get to postpone because of weather; a referee doesn't blow a whistle and cry "foul" if the wind shifts or someone horns in on your hunt; you don't get the chance for a do-over (like three strikes in baseball, or four downs in football) and when you screw up, you don't get the chance to apologize to make things right. Once you pull the trigger, it's final.

Those who prefer to hunt the hard way will also develop some self-reliance skills. When you are in the deep woods, you have to learn to figure things out for yourself. Those skills do come in handy, even in our insulated world. Although we buy as much insurance as we can afford, to shelter us from the what-ifs, who pulls through the best when natural disasters hit? It's the outdoorsman, who has the clothing, gear and know-how to deal with nature in the raw, until the power comes back on. I feel lucky to have been raised in a culture where all that stuff came as second nature. Of course we took care of ourselves, we had to, there was no other way.

A perfect example was the time Brian Edinger broke his leg, while we were making deer drives with the crew in 2005. While his leg was between some roots, he'd lost his balance and snapped it just above the ankle. By the time we got everyone back together, he was hurting pretty good. (It turned out to be a complex fracture. Luckily, no bones were sticking out.) At first he thought he could get between two guys, with his arms around their shoulders and hobble out of the woods. As soon as he moved that leg we knew that plan wouldn't work. Brian's a tough guy, but the grinding of bones against tissue was way too much.

There was a short lapse of time, while we struggled to formulate a plan B. I guess, because I was the oldest, everyone started looking at me. I remember wishing someone else would take charge, but after a few seconds, it became clear to me what we would have to do. We'd have to build a stretcher and carry him out, much the same as we used to carry out moose quarters. It never occurred to any of us to go for help and wait for EMTs to arrive.

So the boys sprang into action, hunting up dead poles to build a frame. They stuck them in between two trees growing close together, breaking them into the right lengths. I was looking for some straight pieces of wood to fashion a splint with, when I came across a good-sized tag alder that had split perfectly straight down the center. I broke the two pieces into equal lengths about a foot long.

Back together; everyone started coughing up building material. Twine, rope, belts, suspenders, hunting jackets and sweatshirts all went into the pile. I showed them the knot I used to lash cross-bucks together for a wall tent and while they were tying the frame together, I went to

48

work applying the splint.

The only knowledge I had on splinting broken bones was what I'd seen on TV shows plus some first aid training for an elk hunting guides license. I centered the alder splints on each side of the break, flat side against the leg, using belts to lash them as tight as Brian could stand it.

Once the frame was ready, we used hunting clothes for padding. We had someone, who would match Brian's 230 pounds, lie on the stretcher while we bounced it up and down, making sure it would hold. Once Brian was loaded, we put a few more jackets on top to keep him warm and with three guys on each side, started carrying him out. Luckily, it was only about a mile to the truck.

Even with the splints, Brian would moan with every little bump. It became obvious to me he wouldn't enjoy the trip to the hospital in the back of a pickup, so I sent two guys ahead to call for an ambulance. I also was concerned about Brian going into shock, which I kept to myself. He responded "No" every time I asked him if he felt sick or was getting cold.

Our neighbor, first responder Connie Wang, was waiting for us when we got to the road. She put oxygen on Brian and I could see it helped him relax. Shortly, the ambulance arrived with one of the EMTs carrying some splinting material, which she laid to the side. We transferred Brian onto a real stretcher and while they prepared to load him I asked, "Aren't you going to put a real splint on?" I could just see the emergency room doctor taking one look at what I had fashioned and wondering, "What cave man put this on?" She responded, "No, I'm not touching that. You guys did an awesome job!"

Because the break was so severe, he ended up going all the way to Marshfield. Despite the lowly tag alder slabs and belts holding it all together, the doctor later told Brian, "Whoever put that on sure knew what he was doing!" Every time Brian tells that story, we have a good laugh.

There is one event that happened many years ago that I have shared with only a few. I was down in the big woods, our traditional hunting country, a place my dad had first shown me. It was one of those soft evenings during deer season, one of those drop-dead quiet times. Not a breath of air was moving, complete and utter calm and stillness. The quiet is so loud you can actually hear it! Some say it's when you can hear the sound of blood rushing through your head. I say it's when you can hear the universe expanding, echoes from the big bang.

So as darkness fell, I headed out, at peace with everything, wishing it would last a little longer. By the time I reached the flat along the river, it was pretty dark; dark enough that at a distance, if you looked straight at something you couldn't make it out, you had to look to the side. As I rounded a bend in the trail, I could make out a manly form with his right shoulder leaning against a big white oak. He appeared to be waiting for me. I thought I was the only one down there that night. Only a relative would have been waiting for me in such a place and no one was supposed to be there and yet, here was someone waiting for me. Feeling a mixture of apprehension and wonderment, I drew near. The man straightened himself from the tree and recognition came as I made out the dark, wide mustache and wide brimmed hat that he wore. From old photos I'd seen many times, I knew it was my great-grandfather. The odd thing about this, you see, is that Great-Grandpa died fifteen years before I was born! As I came alongside he said in a quiet, reassuring voice, "Let's go home." Not knowing what to say, instinctively feeling like a reply would break the spell, I stepped past. He swung in behind and followed the hundred yards or so to the river. As I was stepping off the bank into the riffles to start across, I felt him leave. I turned to see if I could spot him, to wave goodbye, but he was gone.

It was years before I told anyone this story. Before I could feel comfortable telling anyone else, I needed to figure it out for myself why it happened and what it meant. I think the purpose of his visit was to validate my conduct as a hunter. He approved of my efforts to continue to hunt the hard places and keeping alive most of the old ways. He was saying that he had started all of this and was pleased that I was carrying on his legacy. What better place to meet up with me than in our ancestral hunting country, along the river that our family has such deep ties to. Perhaps it was the only place that we could meet.

I guess my mind had, for a little while that quiet evening, been able to tune out the clutter of normal living and instead tune into myself and into the natural rhythms of the earth and heavens. His visit helped bolster my natural resistance to advertising and technology and I became more aware of how important my life is, linking the past to the future. He made me feel that I belonged in wild places and advocating for their continuance was vital, not just for myself, but for others who are or will be seeking more out of life than just material things.

In the routine of our daily lives, we are pounded by the inescapable advertising telling us that if we would just buy their product we would be richer, look better, smell better, play better, hunt better, and be admired because we have the best. The list is endless and the noise becomes so loud, it begins to sound like running water to a beaver, making us crazy and driving us into long hours of labor to stop the noise. We grub for the money and buy the stuff, getting instant gratification but never finding real happiness.

That's what I believe Henry David Thoreau meant when he said, "In wildness is the salvation of the world." Where else but in quiet, wild places can you contemplate what the important things in life are and what is the real meaning of life? For me, the basic important things are; what's the weather right now and what's for supper tonight.

The meaning of life can be a bit more complicated. On TV one time I heard Gorbachev, the former President of Russia, tell a folk story about this young czar who came to power. He gathered all the scholars in the land and instructed them to discover the meaning of life. Over the years, their reports were too thick to read and so he continued to press them to condense it down. Lying on his deathbed, at the end of his long life, he finally received the report he was looking for. Just six words. "You're born. You suffer. You die!" That may be true for some people, but my insides revolt against that finding. My condensed version of the meaning of life is simply to live, really live, not just breathe air and take up space!

The world would be better off if we all had a quiet place where we could ponder such questions. Everyone could use a place where they can meet up with themselves alone, to rediscover what they think, what they feel. Having spent weeks and months in the wilds of Alaska, Montana, and Idaho since the spirit of Great-Grandpa visited me, it has all become clearer. For the well being of the human race, we need to preserve the places where you can hear the universe expanding.

Chapter 6

BRUDDIES

There is a special bond between guys who hunt together. There can be a special bond between brothers. I had both with Larry; we were brothers and buddies. Although we were ten years apart and different in so many ways, I couldn't have asked for a better brother while I was growing up. He didn't like doing things by himself, so he either enjoyed my company or he just liked bossing me around. Either way, I never missed a chance to go hunting, fishing, or trapping with him. He was a "goer" and usually did everything all out. No shortcuts. My dad complained that he walked too fast so you can imagine the effort I had to put forth to keep up when I was ten and he was twenty. That was the first of many times that he got me really tired.

It was beaver trapping season and in those days, there were few beaver in the country. Our dad had told Larry where there might be a beaver pond way west of The Falls. Like I said before, I was a runt growing up. At the end of fifth grade my report card says I was 4'4" and weighed sixty-two pounds. Because The Falls Road wasn't plowed, we would have to snowshoe all the way from County N.

I used a shorter, slightly wider snowshoe, called the Maine style, while Larry used the Alaskan style, a long narrow shoe with high upturned toes. My snowshoes were only two inches shorter than I was. We left the truck about 9:00 and headed west, crossing The Falls on the ice and continuing on. Larry was breaking trail and we walked for what seemed like a long time when we found the old pond. It wasn't alive. Well, we still had a lot of daylight left so he thought maybe there was a pond on Wolf Creek, wherever that was. So we took off again, heading southeast. On the way we got tangled up in a big tag alder swamp. It was hard going in there and my little legs were getting really tired. When we finally found Wolf Creek there was barely half an hour of daylight left. He told me to stay there while he made a quick jaunt upstream to see if there were any beaver up there. It was typical Larry, he never showed up early, was seldom on time, but he never quit early either. By the time he returned it was dark. With snow reflecting the starlight and a skinny crescent moon, the going wasn't too bad as we headed east towards the Steve's Creek hogsback. Well after dark, we made the steep climb up to the top of the ridge and I rolled over the hard snow bank onto the plowed road. The first few steps without my snowshoes on felt like my knees were going to hit me in the chin! It was still two miles back to the truck. Boy, was I tuckered out!

That was the first time I had my doubts that I was going to make it. There really wasn't any other option but to just keep putting one foot in front of the other. After a minnie adventure like that, I had the option to either wise up and quit going along or to believe in myself that I could do it. I ended up choosing the latter.

That was the beginning of a lot of beaver trapping with him. Snowmobiles had not become popular yet, so he and I put an awful lot of snowshoe miles on together. I developed a steady, swinging gait and by the time I was fourteen, I was breaking trail most of the time. By then I still only weighed eight-two pounds so he carried the traps and the ice chisel, while all I carried was the ax. He liked the ponds the farthest back, more time walking but less competition from the other trappers.

There was this one time, while we were setting on a pond northwest of Hawkins, when another trapper came in. We ended up hiking out together. Larry took the lead, then me, then the other guy. He was having a hard time keeping up, I could tell by his heavy breathing. After a while he piped up, "That kid sure can handle those snowshoes!" My head started to swell until Larry came back with, "Ya, he does all right." Typical Larry again, expecting me to keep up, never throwing me a bone or cutting me any slack. I can't ever remember him saying that something might

Moose hunting in Canada in 1972. Larry, me, and cousin Jack Thorsen.

be too heavy for me to handle or too hard to do. Instead, what I had grown to expect was, "When I was your age," followed by some mighty feat, like carrying a 100-pound milk can out of the milk house, one in each hand! I learned to give 110 percent all the time.

I got a little revenge once, with the help of my dad. We started moose hunting in Canada while I was in my early 20's. Typical of the way we always hunted, we motored way up a river to a big lake where we set up camp. From there we portaged a couple canoes way back into a chain of small lakes. I'd found a place the farthest back and had killed a small bull the first day. The next morning we all went to get him out; my dad, our cousin, Jackie Thorsen, Larry and I. After we got all four quarters loaded in the canoe it was still riding fairly high. So, my dad thought all four of us could get in too. Well, Larry wanted no part in that until Pop promised to stay along the shore all the way around to the opposite side where the next portage was. Once under way, with Dad in front and me in the back, we had less than an inch of freeboard, but the lake was really calm. It wasn't long before Dad said, "Aw hell, cut 'er across Gary." Larry started protesting like crazy but there wasn't a thing he could do. The next thing I knew he had taken off his life jacket and tied it on to his gun! I never did understand the reasoning behind that. I guess he didn't want his gun to drown. We couldn't con him into anymore overloaded trips after that.

My brother Larry in front of Lawrence Wang, carrying out a moose quarter in 1966 in Canada.

I did earn some real respect from him on a later hunting trip up there. There were six of us that time, Tom Bader and Lawrence Wang having joined us. We had killed two moose together right after the second portage, which was the longest, about three-quarters of a mile. My dad had come up with a system of fabricating a stretcher on the spot, on which a quarter of meat at a time was placed, and two men would carry it out. My brother-in-law, Tommy Henderson, had experience moose hunting while living in Alaska, and he swore you could pack out moose quarters on a pack frame. I wanted to try it, so I borrowed his, which wasn't too fancy, just a wooden frame with canvas laced over it. I added a strap, which fastened to the top of the frame and went over my forehead, to try and take some of the load off my shoulders.

As I was tying a hindquarter onto my frame, Dad was almost

constantly complaining to me, "You can't do it, forget it." All I would say was, "I just want to try." When Lawrence and Larry helped hoist the pack onto my back, Dad got even more insistent, "Put it down, it's too much Gary." It was really heavy but that was like pouring gas on a fire, I wasn't about to quit now. So I started out.

Of course, by now, I was fully-grown, which still wasn't much – 5'8" and always around 150 pounds. The hindquarters came in right around 100 pounds and by the time I reached the top of the hill, coming up off the lake, I was disappointedly thinking that Tommy was nuts and my dad was right. But level ground made a tremendous difference and it wasn't long before I started feeling better. I stopped to rest

"Put it down, Gary. It's too much."

once, about halfway out, and was careful to set the bottom of the pack on top of a log, while I rested, so I could get up again. On the way back I met Larry, Lawrence and Tommy taking turns on the stretcher, carrying out a front quarter (with the ribs attached, they were a lot bulkier). By the time they'd carried out the four front quarters, I had carried out the four hindquarters. It took me six stops to make the last trip. I sure slept good that night! Although he never told me, I learned through others that Larry thought that was quite a feat.

Through other experiences similar to this, I was learning that doing something difficult is as much mental as it is physical. It was beginning to look like if I wanted to do something bad enough, then I would find a way and the will to do it!

Larry was part of another enlightening moment in my life. As I said before, after the boating accident when I was six, I didn't set foot in another boat until I was twelve. He was responsible. Larry was trapping muskrats with a little duck boat down on the flowage and the first day I stayed on shore. It sure was boring. After an awful lot of pestering to come along on the second day, I gave in and climbed aboard. We weren't twenty yards from the bank when I was wondering what the heck I was afraid of. I learned then to face my fears. No more would I let an accident or silly fears stop me from experiencing life.

We had many more adventures together, from elk hunting in the West to deer hunting around home. As adults, we liked each other, although we were different in many ways. He saw things more black and white; I saw more gray. He liked country and western; I liked rock and roll. He combed his hair just so; I figured that's what hats were for. His stuff was always clean and polished; I could care less what things look like as long as they work. He'd feel bad if his gunstock got a scratch in it; I figured it added character. He preferred company; I didn't mind being alone. But we hunted well together. I don't ever remember a really strong disagreement between us or ever being mad at each other. There was this mutual respect where we understood each other's strengths and weaknesses. If he thought I was better at something, he would let me take the lead and vice versa. I wouldn't say he was a jovial person, a real hoot to be around, but he wasn't always serious either. He had a pretty even keel, except there was this one time…

We were down in Milwaukee for a family wedding. I can't remember why, but we went to this great big shopping mall called Southridge. We got to wandering around in there gawking at this and that when suddenly he stopped, turned to me real serious like and said, "I wish I'd brought my hatchet along so I could blaze a few corners." The thought of two country bumpkins wandering the halls of a shopping mall, chipping paint off corners so they could find their way back out, still makes me laugh.

We continued on through this concrete and steel wilderness and came to a pair of escalators. It was early on a Saturday morning, at least early for city folk, so hardly anyone was around. He spotted that escalator coming down and said, "Did you ever try running up one of these things? It's really hard!" Before I could say anything, a grin came across his face and he said, "Race you to the top," and took off. Even though he had a head start, I figured I could take him and took off after him.

Often, perfect timing is what makes an experience memorable. Wouldn't you know it, as we started up an older lady got on up top. As we approached she crowded over to the side to get out of our way, but the look she was giving us! Larry, undaunted, shouts to her as he went by, "Hey lady, do you know how to make these stairs stop moving?" Of course he won. I was laughing too hard!

Larry never was much for compliments but he had this little grin, which told you, "good job". Only twice can I think of him paying me a real compliment. A few years after high school, I started playing on a fast pitch softball team for Kennan. I have a little natural talent, but I have to practice a lot to be very good. My boyhood friend, Lee Arndt, and I spent many hours practicing together. I would hit him ground balls at third base, then while I played in short, out in left field, he would pound fly balls deep over my head so I could practice catching them. A few years later, I'm trying to play baseball on the Prentice team with Larry. That day he was in center and I was in left. The batter hit a high fly ball deep in the gap between us. Just like I'd practiced and done many times before, I turned, tucked my head, and headed for the fence. Once I got up to cruising speed, I looked back over my right shoulder and found the ball. It was still flying deep. I didn't think I could catch up with it, but at the final stride, on a dead run, I thought "maybe," and stuck my glove up. It was a true Willie Mays catch! Larry had been running over to back me up and he just couldn't contain himself. "Nice catch! Nice catch!"

The other time, we were making deer drives with our family hunting gang, about twelve of us. We had stopped to eat our lunch under a grove of hemlock and, like usual, scattered around in small groups. Larry was in with a little group including cousins Brian and Travis Edinger. They had grown up in a very rough and tumble family and some of those boys had carried it on into adulthood. For instance, as kids they would have water fights, not with squirt guns like normal kids but with water buckets. Once the bucket was empty, they would fling those at each other! Just a few years earlier, Travis and I had been talking about some fistfights he's been in, and finally I asked him why. A pleasant grin came over his face as he explained, "When you knock a guy on his ass, some jerk who really deserves it, it feels as good as having sex!"

So, in their little group, they started telling stories about family members and the crazy and rough things they had done. The conversation took a slight turn towards who they thought was the toughest. Finally Larry chimed in, "I'll tell you, pound for pound, I'll put Gary up against anyone! I don't mean in a fight, but just plain tough. He just won't quit!"

Wow, now that was a compliment! I was behind him quite a ways and I don't think he knew I could hear him. I immediately thought to myself, "If I am tough Larry, it's because of you."

In early 2004 Larry was diagnosed with stomach and lung cancer. Although he had never smoked, he had been having these coughing fits for a long time. When I would tell him he needed to get that checked, he would just shrug it off. The first time I saw him after the diagnosis he said, "Man, when they tell you you have cancer that sure sucks it out of ya." He was an over the road trucker most of his life and the last few years he'd been running extra hard, trying to build up his retirement. He had put off doing some things until after retirement and I told him that was going to be a real kick in the pants if this didn't turn out right.

He underwent heavy doses of chemo and the tumors shrank for a while, but by early fall he was going back to the hospital more and more often, just like Mom had done. Just before I left on my annual elk hunt out west, Betty and I went to visit him in the hospital. He was pretty sick that afternoon but we all expected him to be released in a few days. As I left all I said was, "See ya." and he said, "Have a good hunt." I so wished I was taking him along.

I drove out to Montana with a horse and two mules and a friend packed me back into a wilderness area. He took the stock out the next day because there was no graze where I camped. I'd told my wife Leanne and sister Betty that if something bad happened to Larry not to try to get a hold of me. It would take a major undertaking by someone to get a message to me.

After seven days of hunting I hiked out of the hills. When I called home that night there was bad news. Larry had taken a dramatic turn for the worse. The doctors had given him only a few days to live, and that was four days ago. Typical Larry, he was not going to be on time, even for his own death.

Well, I had to get camp out, so I headed back in with the stock the next day. It was a sad trip. After I had eaten supper and packed up everything I could, there was still a little daylight left. Next to camp was this great big boulder, the size of a living room, on the shore of the lake. If you have enough squirrel in you, you can get up on top of it. It was a very calm contemplative evening as I sat on that rock, not enjoying the beautiful evening because I was feeling so blue. Suddenly, a sound I had never heard before in the Lower Forty-eight drifted down the steep forested ridge to me. The wild, lonesome howl from the timber wolf only deepened my sorrow.

A few minutes later he called again, and I thought how perfectly his long, mournful sound was reflecting my own feelings. When the wolf howled a third time, it came to me, perhaps he's grieving with me, two fellow hunters mourning the loss of another. We three were so alike. Top predators actively engaged in the circle of life. We needed to hunt to be alive. We needed wild places to hunt in, the farther from civilization, the better; places of noninterference from others not of our clan. For me, I could not have been in a better place at such a time. Alone, along side a high mountain lake in the middle of the wilderness with a wolf sent to help me mourn. As darkness settled in around us, the wolf called one more time. The best brother and hunting partner I could have ever asked for was dying. I sat on the rock and quietly wept.

I packed out the next day. When I got to the trailhead, I just threw everything in the truck and trailer and headed home. That night, while I was somewhere crossing North Dakota, Larry took his last breath.

I was glad I'd made it back for the funeral. Someone said it was too bad I didn't get back in time to say good-bye. Oddly, I didn't feel that way. There really wasn't anything we needed to say. We knew each other so well, the good and the bad. We had been in so many tight spots together and had never let each other down. Had never quit. He knew I had such a deep, abiding sense of friendship and respect for him and I know he felt the same about me. For one of us to have said, "I love you man," well that would have embarrassed the hell out of both of us.

As I tuned out the preacher droning on about things I didn't believe in, I found myself remembering Larry's distinctive sound as he gave the owl hoot, the Edinger's hunting call. The call imitates the hooting of a Barred Owl. Bird books say it sounds like, "Who cooks for you?" For us it means "come here" or "where are you," depending on the circumstance. I started fantasizing about standing up at the end of the service and giving Larry one last hunting call. I wanted to so badly but I knew I couldn't pull it off; I was choking up just thinking about it. I'd wished I had thought about it earlier and asked one of my cousins to do it. Many in the audience would have thought it was strange, but the relatives would have understood. After all, hunting is one of the main things that holds this family together. One last hunting call. A final goodbye. It would have been a wonderful and fitting tribute to a real hunter from his hunting kin. I still miss him terribly.

Chapter 7

RACING DOGS

In my living room there is a shelf, above the picture window, which runs from wall to wall. On it are crowded trophies from nineteen years of racing sled dogs. They overflow onto the mantle above the fireplace and used to hang on walls and stand in corners, but more important things, like family photos and kid's toys, have pushed many aside. If my memory is correct, Leanne and I had brought home 126 trophies from New Hampshire, New York, Michigan, Wisconsin, Minnesota, and Wyoming; the Canadian Provinces of Manitoba, Saskatchewan, Alberta, British Columbia, Yukon and on into Alaska. Some races were generous and gave out trophies down to fifth place; others were stingier and only gave out to second or third.

An awful lot of memories are within those trophies. The exhilarating feeling of triumph, of so many special dogs, and a very few very special friends. They are a testament to literally thousands of hours of caring for and training dogs, a single-minded determination to be one of the best. How does a kid from Wisconsin become a dog musher? I was just following a dream.

After Mom died and high school graduation, I stayed at home and took over farming for the family. Dad was no farmer, so Peggy and Jerry and I kept things going around the house. But I had this burning desire to get away from the nest and follow the footsteps of my older siblings, so I headed for Milwaukee in March of 1970. My sister Nancy and her husband Ken said they had an extra bedroom and I could live with them, paying a small fee for rent.

Gary Chase, a high school friend who would later be best man at my wedding, was already working at a small factory in West Allis, so I stopped there one day. The supervisor said something about kids from Up North knowing how to work and hired me on the spot for $3.25 an hour. I quickly adjusted to life in the city.

Early that summer, a friend of a friend of Nancy's had a female husky they wanted to give away. I'd always wanted a dog team. Growing up,

I had read *"Call of the Wild"* and *"White Fang"* by Jack London and had fantasized about having my own trap line team. Aha! The beginnings of a dog team. I picked her up and early that summer, when she came in heat, another friend of a friend gave me the phone number of a guy by Green Bay, named Kent Allender, who actually raced sled dogs. Nine weeks after my trip up there, I had the makings of my dog team, seven puppies.

I was surprised to learn that there were sled dog races in Wisconsin. Kent urged me to join the Wisconsin Trailblazers Sled Dog Club and to come to a race that winter. When I told him I just wanted a pleasure team he replied, "I'll bet you will be racing before too long." I wonder how he knew?

I did go to see a race that January and saw what it all looked like: sleds, harnesses, ganglines, snow hooks. Most of all, I came away with the idea that, "Shoot, I can do that!" I was hooked. The next weekend was a race at Kalkaska, Michigan, which is just below the Mackinaw Bridge. I ended up leaving Friday evening, driving all night so I could watch the race on Saturday and then drove back to Milwaukee that night. I really had it bad now.

Nancy lived out in the country, on the south side of the city. I built a sled and started training my pups, using the ditch along 76th street and the neighbor's farm field. Pretty soon, I was making the five-hour trip to Kennan every weekend and training up there. I didn't have a clue what I was doing, but by hook and by crook and pure instinct I got those pups running pretty good.

I stayed in touch with Kent through the next summer and early that fall I took my team over there to show them off. He was so impressed by the way my team had run that, a week later, I got a letter from him asking me if I would be interested in being his kennel boy for the season. He wanted me to help his wife, Barb, care for their kennel of sixty dogs and to do much of the training while he was on the road, during the week, as a salesman. In return, I would learn from the top dog musher in Wisconsin and I could travel with him during the race season and race my team in the five-dog class, which was commonly a five-mile run each day. In those days, the five-dog class was the beginner's class.

I talked it over with my oldest sister Betty and her husband Tommy. They had become my surrogate parents after Mom got cancer. I clearly recall Tommy's counsel, "If it's something you really want to do, then do it. You may never get a chance like this again." That was all I needed.

Factory work had become incredibly boring and city life had lost its appeal, there was just nothing to do in Milwaukee!

Kent and I turned out to be a pretty good team. He had a degree in Biology and liked to focus on the science of the sport. Since I was a farm kid, I knew how to handle animals, as a hunter I understood animal instincts and from both I knew how to read animals. As I settled into the fall training routine, it began to feel like I was born to drive dogs.

Our first race was over at Bemidji, Minnesota. It was a major race attracting teams from the east coast all the way to Alaska. At the end of the race, people were all wondering who that new young fella was who had won the five-dog class with a team of yearling pups. To prove it was no fluke, I came in second the next weekend at Ely, Minnesota.

Ely turned out to be a pretty interesting race. Besides being the coldest race I was ever in, (minus 38 degrees when I left the starting chute on Sunday) I got to eat supper with a legend of the sport, Dr. Roland Lombard. Doc Lombard was a veterinarian from Massachusetts who had won every major race in North America, some numerous times. He had also helped the International Sled Dog Racing Association (ISDRA) by serving as its first president in 1966. Although "Doc" wasn't an officer anymore, I think he wanted to talk ISDRA politics with Kent because Kent was then the Vice President of ISDRA, so he invited us to have supper with him and his wife, Louise, that night.

On the way back to the motel, Kent was feeling quite giddy from being in such select company and asked me in a leading manner, "Well Gary, what did you think of Doc Lombard?" "He seemed like a normal man," I said. Holy cow, wrong answer! "Well, he may put his pants on one leg at a time, but there is nothing normal about Doc Lombard! He is one of the greatest mushers to have ever lived! For someone like you to have had the chance to have supper with a legend and call him normal….."

Looking back, I probably should have felt more reverence, but at the same time, it turns out that I judge people more on what kind of person they are than on some gift they were probably born with. For me, calling anyone who engages in the egotistical arena of sports normal is actually quite a compliment. A strong ego is necessary to compete at a high level in any kind of sport, but keeping it under control is very difficult. Many years later, when I reached the top of my sport, I was not comfortable with people wanting to be around me just because I could get sixteen dogs to run down the trail really fast. I wanted people to like me for who I was, as an actual person, not just a dog driver. Many of the friends that remain from my dog racing days never did win a dog race, but there are so many other things in life they have won at.

By the end of that '72 season, our kennel had done pretty well. Barb had been very competitive in the seven-dog class, (in those days the semi-pro class) and Kent ended up winning the Bronze medal in the open (pro class) accumulating the third most points in the ISDRA sanctioned events. Kent wanted me to stay on and together we could build a championship dog team, promising some day I would drive the top team. But someday was too far away and I wanted to call my own shots, so we parted, best of friends. We remained close friends the rest of his life. Many times I commented on how I thought our continued relationship was so odd, since we had so little in common. One day he gave me a book with these words inside the front cover:

To Gary, whom I am privileged to call my friend-
My friend is someone who shares with me
the tranquility of wind whispering through tall pines;
The quiet exhilaration of a dog team running in perfect rhythm;
The bittersweet melancholy
of the huskies' haunting chorus;
The calm power of truth and fairness,
The serenity of a spirit at peace,
The warmth of a good story,
The joy of a good laugh;
The virtues of silence and intelligence,
of trust and respect;
And a bond which asks no due.
What of common ground? It is all of these and more;
A friendship that endures.
W. Kent Allender
April 27, 1988

I headed back to Kennan because I knew that it was a good area to train dogs in; quiet country roads to train on in the fall and dependable snow from December on. I had bought a small trailer house to live in at Kent's, so I could have my own space. I pulled it home and parked it in my dad's yard, which was actually Nancy's and mine now. We had bought the land just to keep it in the family, not knowing at that time that Kennan was where I was going to make my stand.

The next three years I spent in the seven-dog class, which normally ran a ten-mile trail per day. I won a few here and there, but mostly hung around third, fourth, or fifth. Kennan was still a hard place to make a living, so making enough money to support a dog team was quite a task. In summer I worked with my neighbor, Lawrence Wang, doing concrete construction, which proved to be physically hard, hot and dirty work, and in the winter I drove log truck for another neighbor, Jerry Litvinoff. Every hour I worked was so I could get more money to better my dog team. The sport was in the process of taking a giant leap forward when it came to dogs and nutrition. Average speeds jumped from 15 to 18 MPH. over night and we were finding high protein, high fat diets were superior to the normal cereal diet of commercial dog foods.

In April of '75 I got distracted for a little while. My younger brother, Jerry, was dating a girl from Phillips, so they set me up on a blind date with her older sister. She was a senior in high school and as cute as a button. On our first real date, I wanted to take her for a ride with my dog team, what else? (When there is no snow, the dogs pull a fairly heavy three-wheeled training cart with hydraulic brakes that two people can ride on comfortably.) The afternoon of the date, I stopped the pulp truck in front of the grocery store, where she worked as a checkout, and tried to cancel because it was going to be a miserable, cold, wet, windy evening. She insisted we should go anyway. "Well, OK."

We got what I knew we would; cold, wet and splattered by mud kicked up by the dog's feet. But Leanne surprised me. She seemed to enjoy the dogs and never whined about a thing. Barely 100 pounds, dripping wet, I began to think she could handle anything I would throw at her, so I asked her out again. Although she was smart enough to be Valedictorian of her class, she was dumb enough to keep saying yes to another date. We got along so well that, two and a half years later, after she graduated from Technical College as a medical lab technician, we were married. It was the best move I ever made.

At the conclusion of the '75 Ely race, I was sitting with Bruce Christman, waiting for the awards ceremony to begin. He was a musher from out East trying to break into the top of the open class. Out of the blue he asked me, "Do you ever plan to move up into the open class?" When I said I did, he came back with, "Well then, quit wasting your time in the seven-dog. Open racing is not even the same sport, there is just so much more to learn. If the big time is what you're aiming for, then plunge in and do it!"

Well, the next year, I took his advice and promptly ended up in the bottom half of most of the races. I could hold my own against the

Midwest mushers, but as soon as the big boys showed up, I was an also ran. The main problem was the dogs I had. Kent was always trying to tell me, "You can't make a silk purse out of sow's ear." I was getting everything I could out of my dogs, but what they had to give wasn't good enough. Kent had quit the sport by now and had given me his best dogs, but the sport had even gone past their genetic potential.

A couple of lucky breaks came my way in the same year. I was always broke, pouring what I had into paying for dog food and gear and travel expenses. First, Jim Gabrielson of Birchland Realty in Phillips offered to give me some hundreds of dollars as a sponsorship and my boss, Jerry, put together a logging bee for me. He got a bunch of our logging friends together and all the wood they cut that day would be donated to me. There was Jerry, Nick and Norm Runnheim, Ernie Jablonsky, Kevin and Kirby Lebal, Frosty Adomaitas and my brother Larry. That ended up being some more hundreds of dollars. With that money I bought two brood bitches out of Alaska. Blackie was from Bernie Turner and she was already bred to his top-producing stud, Murphy. The other female was a dog named Soul from Dick Brunk. She was out of Junior, a male world-class musher Harvey Drake had bred extensively and had become famous.

Because those two guys were willing to share some top genetic stock with me at a decent price, I was able to climb slowly off dead center. Bernie wasn't known as a top racer – perhaps his ego wasn't big enough – but he had a reputation as a sage in Alaskan racing circles, knowing bloodlines, training secrets, and he had a tremendous eye for good dogs. Dick Brunk was just breaking into the top tier of dog men and would later play into another adventure on the Yukon River. I became good friends with both.

Sled dog racing was supposed to be a wealthy person's game. If a musher wasn't independently wealthy, then a good sponsor was needed. With money you could buy good dogs from top kennels, especially when they quit the sport and sold out. Money would also buy you the time needed to train dogs and take care of all the details needed to be successful. By now I had figured out that to win, I would have to raise my own. My plan was to use my inherent talent as a trainer, my ability to work hard and to claw my way to the top. When those Alaskan bloodlines, mixed together with Kent's, started making my team as yearlings, it all became clear. All I needed was good dogs. All I needed to do was to keep breeding, proving, and selecting the right genes and winning would happen all by itself. Rewards would come with hard work and patience.

Looking back now, I don't know how Leanne and I managed to do it. I was putting in fifty to sixty hours a week driving pulp truck and Leanne was working a normal forty-hour job. Somehow we squeezed in caring for and training a kennel that had now grown to around 100 animals, counting puppies and breeding stock. On top of that, we somehow managed to build our own log home on the back forty, which turned out to be a three-year "spare time" project. From the ridge our house sits on, we can see where my Great-Grandparents had lived. Youth, determination, and sheer will got us through.

Late in the season of '76, I did a really stupid thing. When I woke up that Tuesday morning, I could feel a slight pain in my right side but I chose to ignore it and headed for work. By the time I got to Catawba with the pulp truck, I knew something was seriously wrong and turned around and went home. I lay in bed for a while until the pain got so bad I called Betty. We both figured I had appendicitis so she sent Tommy down to haul me off to the Medford Hospital. All the way down he told me stories of people who had died from a burst appendix! They rushed me into surgery and when I came to, the surgeon told me they had caught it just in time. When they turned me loose on Thursday, they said I was supposed to take it easy for six weeks.

Well, I was entered at a small race at Glidden, Wisconsin, that weekend and because Leanne didn't have enough experience yet to race my open team, I asked my brother Jerry to run them for me. On Saturday my team came in second. They should have been in first, but it wasn't Jerry's fault the team wouldn't listen to him. Since I was tilting only a little to the right when I walked, I made up my mind to race them on Sunday. We were too far out of first to have a realistic chance at winning, (final standings are determined by total elapsed time) but I wanted to prove that I had a good dog team. Sunday would have worked out just fine, except that I flipped the sled once and when I was dragging (you never let go, the team just keeps going) I really put a lot of stress on those fresh stitches. I did have the fastest time that day and so the Edinger pride was restored. Looking back, it was a crazy and dangerous game I played that day.

Over the next ten years I improved every year. 1986 was the finest year I had. By now, all I'm doing from the end of December until April is racing dogs, making my winter living off the purse money. I have a core group of twenty-two dogs to make up a sixteen-dog team; six of them are leaders I rotate over the season. Leanne is racing our second open team using the six I'm not running that weekend and giving experience to our best yearlings to fill out her twelve-dog team. We have two brothers, Grit and Swaps, that have shown great promise as leaders, so I have taken my time with them, never putting too much pressure on them too early. At two and a half years of age, now is the time to see what they got.

Bemidji, Minnesota, was a one-day race because of weather. I came in second. My racing style and strategy by now is to always make my move on the second day, if I have to. I need to do well at every race, not win at the cost of jeopardizing the next race or the rest of the season. At Ely I won, my first major win. Just before the finish line, the trail came off the lake and climbed a steep hill. I'd learned to always call up the team, at the end of the first day, to see if there were any weak dogs in the team to leave out the next day. Just before the end of the lake I called them up, asking them what they had left after fifteen miles. I can still feel the handle bar leap forward as all sixteen dogs leaned into their harnesses and we charged all the way into the finish line. Wow, these guys were really something!

On Sunday I left the line second, with the fastest teams from the day before going out first at two minute intervals. For the first time in a race, I put Grit and Swaps together in lead. Usually my team would scream out of the starting chute before settling into a more sustainable pace about two miles out. This day, they just kept going; my young leaders were setting a blistering pace. At the thirteen-and-a-half-mile mark a two-and-one-half-year-old female, Mandy, went down. She wasn't that tired; she just decided she'd had enough that day. I hit the brake and set the hook (anchor) in the lake ice in one quick motion.

As I raced forward to unhook Mandy to load her in the sled, I felt the pressure of seconds slipping away. The seconds turned out to be very precious because at the end of this race, after thirty-two miles of racing, a mere sixty-nine seconds separated the top nine teams. There was added pressure because I knew the hook in the lake ice was not set very deep. The team will normally only give you fifteen to twenty seconds before they become impatient, jumping and lunging into their harness to get going again. On the way back to the sled, just as I reached the last pair of dogs in front of the sled (wheel dogs) the team popped the hook. With Mandy in my right hand, I just barely had time to hook the driving bow with my left elbow as it was going by, knowing if I tried to grab it with just one hand, I'd never be able to hang on. I tried to gracefully swing aboard, but it didn't work and the sled flipped on its side with us dragging behind. Somehow I managed to get the sled upright and got my knees on the runners so I could swing the dog into the basket. (Lucky that it wasn't one of the bigger males) As I stood up, I saw we had drifted off the trail to the left and were on a false snowmobile track. I hollered "Gee" and jammed on the brake. Swaps jerked Grit to the right and I said, "All right." As we angled back onto the race trail, Grit was going to continue angling across onto another false trail. At the same time I hollered "Haw," Swaps rammed Grit hard with his left shoulder, throwing him straight down the track. We finished without further incident. When they added up the times, my second and sixth day placings added up to first. I couldn't believe it! Swaps had won the race for me, with twenty-one seconds to spare.

The next race was the Alpo International at Saranac Lake, New York. It had the biggest payout of all the races that year, a whopping $6,000 for first place. The oddest thing happened just after we pulled into the race site on Saturday morning and were dropping dogs. (Dropping means letting them out of their boxes and clipping them around the truck on short chains) All of a sudden there was this exclamation behind me, "I can't believe it!" I whirled around and there was Bruce Christman, who I hadn't seen since he had told me to jump into the open class eleven years before at Ely. I said, "Hi Bruce," and stuck out my hand but he just ignored me, staring at my dogs and started saying, "It's them, it's them!" with this incredulous look on his face. So now I'm totally confused and finally he looks at me and explains, "I had a dream last night that a team of black dogs won this race and they looked exactly like these! It's them! It's them!" he repeated.

The majority of my dogs' color went back to a dog named Rowdy, who was coal black with spotted white feet, a throwback to some Belgian Shepherd blood. It was a dominant gene that carried on to succeeding generations. Also from Kent's lines was a streak of greyhound from eastern Canada, which gave them the racy body form I was looking for; fine-boned, long-legged dogs that looked fast just standing still. When I threw in Soul, from Dick Brunk whose line was famous for this craziness to run, it all came together. Those were the dogs that had caught Bruce's eye. Should I dare to believe his dream would come true?

The first day I put Grit and Swaps at lead again, because they had done so well at Ely and because the trail was hard packed and fast. We had a good solid run and when the times were posted I was in 1st place, a mere 13 seconds ahead of Doug McRae, a fellow Wisconsin musher from Rhinelander. It snowed quite a bit that night and although the trail crew did all they could to prepare the track for Sunday, I knew it would be a sloppy trail. I put Swaps in lead with his mother, Amy, who was out of the female from Bernie Turner. Amy preferred a slower pace going out, so I could use her today, but I knew how tough she was and in case I had to drive (push) the dogs coming home, I knew she would stay on the trail and power through the slop.

The 13.5-mile trail was a straight abandoned railroad grade that went out, had a four-mile loop on the end, and came back in on itself, so there was head on passing. Normally these open teams are very professional, practically ignoring other teams. If I had a dog pay any attention to any distraction, people, horses, stray dogs, even a squirrel, all I had to do was speak their name in a serious tone and their mind would come right back to business.

On the way back in, everything was going perfectly until we met one of the later starting teams on their way out. For quite a ways I could see trouble headed my way in the form of one of his dogs pulling way out, wanting to hide in my dog team, not wanting to go. I don't know why the driver kept coming like that, my team was crowded over to the right as far as it could get. I slowed my team down and had my snow hook ready when that miserable dog piled into my leaders. Before my team dogs could overrun my front end, I had the hook in and was running up to untangle dogs. All I could see was $6,000 slipping away and I just started swearing, not at the other musher, not even at his dogs, just about the whole situation. By the time I got up there, more of his dogs were trying to hide among mine. I just started throwing dogs out of my team. I didn't care where they landed, as long as they weren't in mine! I got everybody clear, pulled my leaders out straight again and ran back to the sled and jerked the hook out. My dogs were more than happy to get out of there and when I looked back, the other team was in an awful mess. I didn't feel bad; none of it was my fault.

The rest of the way in, if it looked to Amy and Swaps like there was going to be any more trouble, they would swing out into the deeper snow, giving everything a wide berth. Even with the trouble that day, we won handily, almost two minutes ahead of second place. These guys sure could run. Bruce's dream had become reality.

Flush with cash, we headed back to the Midwest where the next race was Grand Rapids, Minnesota. At the end of the first day, I was thirty-eight seconds behind Joee Redington of Alaska. That was actually a lot of time to make up, but I had been second in this race four years in a row. I foolishly decided to win this race, so once again I put Grit and Swaps in lead on Sunday, planning on making up the time. At about the nine-mile mark of the thirteen-mile race, the trail ran down a powerline. I spotted Joee just turning off the powerline so I looked at my watch and when I got to the same place about a minute and a half had expired. At that point we were about even for the race. The rest of the trail was quite hilly, so I never got a time on Joee again. At the eleven-mile mark, the first time I used it all year, I cracked the signal whip, using that little edge of fear to ask for everything they had. There was no question in their mind what I wanted and they dug in hard, heading for the finish line.

Just before the finish line was a snow fence blocking a side trail. In the middle of the snow fence was a small hole at the bottom. As we flew past, Grit looked at it. That's all he did, never faltered, never wavered, just looked at it. When we got back to the truck, the first thing I said to Leanne was, "I think I screwed up Grit." I did win the race by sixteen seconds but I had found the mental limit of Grit. After that, if I planned to drive the team hard, I couldn't have Grit at lead, he would "duck," purposely take the wrong trail to escape the pressure. Grand Rapids was not a race worth "blowing up" one of your best leaders over, but I had made the choice and it was done. Like most things in life, you can't go back and have a do over. You have to learn from it and go on. I never was much for crying over spilled milk anyway.

Another reason I went for it at Grand Rapids was that the next three races were smaller, ten-dog affairs. Leanne took the best dogs and came in second at Shawano, Wisconsin, before I hit the road by myself, winning at Prince Albert, Saskatchewan, and Edmonton, Alberta. The next real test was Fort McMurray, Alberta, which I had won the year before. Besides hoping to do well, I wanted to use it as a shakedown run to prepare for the North American Championship in Fairbanks, Alaska, two weeks afterward. McMurray was two twenty-mile heats while Fairbanks, a three-day race, was twenty miles on Friday and Saturday with a thirty-mile run on Sunday. I won fairly easily at McMurray. At the sixteen-mile mark I remembered the first time I'd raced here, two years earlier. We had had a very poor showing, coming in next to last. None of the dogs had ever gone past sixteen miles before and when we reached that spot, you could just see the whole team wondering where the finish line was, wondering if they could run any further. I knew exactly how they were feeling, remembering that snowshoe trek with Larry when I was ten.

Feeding dogs on the Alaska Highway.

It's hard to have a dog team prepared to win any race from thirteen to thirty miles. Once they have gone twenty-plus miles, many dogs will start saving a little for the next long run, not knowing when that may occur. To prepare to win the North American, I figured a person would have to have a bunch of long training runs on them. They would probably get sour, not even wanting to leave the truck, but you would have to stay on them, making them go until they accepted the runs as just another day at the office. That would build their confidence in themselves and in me. The trick is not to betray their confidence, knowing what their limit is without going beyond it. All running contests are like that, always pushing the extreme limits without going over the edge. The problem with long training, as I have been trying to allude to, is that it is then very difficult to get them to go all out in a fourteen-mile race. Like I said before, I needed to do well in every race so I could afford to continue racing. The shorter races in the Lower Forty-eight were my bread and butter and that's what my breeding program was aimed at. My plan for Fairbanks was to pretty much let the dogs run their race, and let the chips fall where they may.

I finished fourth at Fairbanks and was satisfied with that. I figured I hadn't hurt the team for next year. Looking back, I probably should have gone for it. Sometimes things just come together by accident, like leaders and the age of the dogs and fall training conditions; things you can't control. Obviously, things came together for me in 1986. Our kennel had accomplished a feat very few ever have, a second and a fourth with nothing but wins in between. And we were blue-collar mushers on top of it, not having a major sponsor or independent wealth or an extended family to help out. The patience, Edinger tenacity and hard work had finally paid off.

The funny thing is, I didn't really realize what we had done. I remember wondering where all the big boys had gone! When I look back through the race results, I was in a crowd of guys who were, or soon became, legends in their time; Redington, McRae, Dunlap, Streeper, Robb, Attla, Saunderson, Erhart. Pretty select company. To cap it off, I was selected "Musher of the Year" by Team and Trail, the foremost mushing publication of the time. I had made it. Thanks to Leanne being beside me every step of the way, I was one of the best!

On the mantle above our fireplace is a black and white photograph of a dog team. All fourteen dogs are strung out beautifully, heads down, tails slung low behind them, all business. Even with their strides frozen in time, you can tell they are really eating up the ground. On the back of the sled, the musher has a heavy parka on and a wide white ear band is snugged down over a baseball cap. The parka's fur ruff is pulled tightly around the back of his neck, framing his shoulders. Over the parka is a white racing bib bearing the number 1, the number everyone else in the race would have gladly traded for that day. He stands lightly but confidently on the runners, a pose that comes naturally after sixteen years and thousands of miles behind a dog team. At the bottom of the photo I have scribbled "1987-Laconia-World Champs!" Under that is third day and the names of all the dogs, so I won't forget, all the black dogs looking the same at this distance. My memory takes me back and again I am standing on the runners.

Although not up to the previous year's standards, I am still having a pretty good year. After finishing fourth at Bemidji, I'd won Ely again (by a mere three seconds), slipped back to my old habit of coming in second at Grand Rapids and finished third at Saranac. This is my first try at winning the World's Championship Dog Derby at Laconia, New Hampshire, and I had picked the perfect year. Laconia is usually a warm race with a snowstorm thrown in sometime during the three days. This year, all three days had been unusually cold, with the track hard and fast.

After Friday's run I was sitting in second. Saturday I had put Grit and Swaps together in lead, not planning to push them at all, just letting them set a fast happy pace. It's easy for the dogs when it's cold. After they posted the times for the second day, race analyzers said I had been crafty for grabbing a nearly insurmountable lead going into the last day. I let them think what they wanted.

As I stare at the picture, I remember how I knew those dogs so well. It felt like I could just reach into their heads and dial them just where I wanted, happy and running free or serious, feeling and knowing my urgency to eat up the ground. We had been in plenty of sobering spots together and had worked out what was expected of them and what I had to do, so they could meet those expectations. I always figured you could take the true measure of a man by standing next to him when the chips were down. That's also true with dogs.

Laconia – 1987, the second day. Swaps (the dark dog) and Grit at lead.

At wheel, just ahead of the sled, are Renegade and Sable. Sable is a really fast dog, but fairly lazy, that's why I keep her close to me. At wheel is the only place that I can count on her giving me a good run every time. Renegade is one of the old troopers. He's not lazy like Sable, but he's figured out that he can run with a little less intensity, and still get back to the finish line soon enough. He never hurts you and I run him all over in the team except the front four.

Ditto for Rebel, Renegade's identical twin, who is running just ahead of wheel today. Rebel has a little more speed but he's not as tough mentally as his brother. Paired with Rebel is a small female named Libby. She always acts like she is not very proud of herself and for a race dog, is unusually shy of people. At a race like this, with hundreds of spectators along the trail, I have to keep her towards the back. She has never been lame and never gone down on me. Usually the spot just ahead of wheel is where you run your weakest dogs, but there are no weak dogs in this bunch.

The third pair up are Hazel and Dawn. Hazel is a little red dog that always has to be in the back half of the team; she just doesn't like it farther up. She's another one that has never been hurt or quit. On some days she can take her time before kicking in and she never did get over being afraid of running under bridges or through culverts. Dawn is a bigger female that will not run for Leanne. She is one of those strange dogs that runs better on the second day and even better on the third, if there is one. Not a flashy dog, I had never found her limit, but she had never pushed herself hard enough to find it either.

In the middle of the team are Amy and Brunk. Like Rebel and

73

Renegade, they are also old troopers, the ones who had pushed aside older veterans as yearlings, they were so good, and had stayed in there, refusing to being replaced. In her day, Amy was quite a leader, tough as nails. The harder I drove her the lower she got to the ground, absolutely would not bolt off the trail, no matter what. She also refused to run for Leanne. She is the only one in the whole bunch I did not breed, but like all the rest, had been born, raised and trained at my place. She's running with Brunk today. He is out of Soul, the female I bought from Dick Brunk of Alaska, hence his name. Brunk had been a main leader for a couple of years. He was so crazy to run, there was never any doubt that you were going to leave the starting chute with him in lead. Not having the best of builds, he didn't have the ability to maintain the top speed; so younger more athletic dogs have taken over his leader spot. He was a very proud male and would have been the dominant dog in the kennel, if I had let him.

Behind the point dogs, first team they would be called in the lineup, are Grit and Cochise. I've talked a lot about Grit already. He is the most athletic dog I've ever owned. Just one hell of a dog! I've seen him come off the thirty-mile run in Fairbanks, take a deep breath and ask if there was anything else to do! His only fault was, when at lead, he would duck if you tried to drive the team. The way to get the most out of Grit was to praise him; stand back there on the runners, clap your hands and tell him what a good boy he was. You could actually see him start to grin, and really pour it on. Cochise is another really fast leader, but she will wear down, especially on a three-day race. I started using her in lead as a yearling, she was that good. Now I use her a lot in lead on the first day, which is where she was with Swaps on Friday. Had she been tough in the head, like Amy, she would have been really impressive.

At point, the spot just behind the leaders, I have Calico and Tory. They have run point all three days in this race. Calico is a sister to Cochise and I can't ever remember her having a bad day, but like her sister, can't handle distance. Her problem is she runs too hard, never learned to back off and coast a little here and there. I've tipped her over at both of the long races at McMurray and Fairbanks. She's strictly a right-handed dog, pulls out too far if she's on the left. Her running mate is Tory, a dog most people would pass over. You could seldom play a tune on her backline, she doesn't drive like Calico, but every day of every race she's there, towards the front end, doing her steady thing.

All the dogs in the front half of the team have to know how to stay out of tangles and if they do get in one, know how to get out of it without stopping. When lines go slack up ahead, these veterans slow down and pull out to their individual side, keeping their necklines and backlines tight while getting away from the center line (mainline) dragging on the ground, trying to snare them. You can't teach them that, the smarter ones just learn that on their own.

At lead today are Toby and Swaps. Toby is the one dog that shouldn't be on this team; he's not fast enough. But nobody ever told him that and he never figured it out for himself. He's just a tough, gutsy little male. He's Leanne's favorite leader and has run for her most of the season, so that makes him a little fresher than the rest of these dogs. He hasn't had the pounding and the pressure the others have had. He also belongs in the old trooper bunch and this is the last time he will run in the big team. His last hurrah will be as a leader on a world championship team. Since I have such a big lead, I put him up today because all I want is a nice steady pace. With the temp's so cold he'll make it fine.

Swaps, brother to Grit, is mentally as tough as his mother, Amy. He's as close to perfect as I've ever had except he will get tired. I never had to load him, he just would never quit, but I've seen him wobbling more than once, by the time we reached the finish line. He has the innate ability to want to stay out of trouble and will do whatever it takes to get out of it. He reacts so quickly in a tight situation that I can't really say he actually thinks, but his instincts have always been right. He has run lead every day of every race this year except one. At the awards ceremony he gets the award for best lead dog.

Many of these dogs would never have made it for other mushers. Many drivers will never keep a dog if they have to load it. I guess I got away with it because I could fit them into situations where they were at their best, pairing them with the right dog and placing them in the team to avoid their weaknesses; temperatures and trail conditions always being a major consideration. I got really good at reading dogs, being able to look into their eyes and seeing what was going on inside their head. Some dogs, like Mandy at the Ely race, did just quit, but I figured it was a lack of confidence in themselves as much as anything. I kept working with those dogs because they had the speed. Mandy helped me win Ely again the next year, running point the first day and in the team on Sunday. She thought about quitting the second day, at the same spot she quit the year before, but with the extra training I had on her, she not only stayed up, but ran hard all the way into the finish line. Dick Brunk said the good dogs would run until they passed out, that's how tough they were. I would add another class, the great dogs, who never tipped over, even in times when the musher was asking too much.

The general consensus among the other drivers was that I really knew my dogs and didn't make many mistakes. Some would try to put pressure on me to force me into making a mistake, but that didn't work. I had come to understand that we could only do our best and it really didn't matter what anybody else was doing. A few drivers would set a high bar for themselves by loudly predicting they were going to win before a race, using that method to push themselves harder. I never really set goals. I used my intense, competitive spirit to push me to the limit.

I pushed it too far a few times, like racing my dogs right after I had my appendix out. Another time I was on my way up the Alaska Highway, trying to pull off one of my normal all-nighters, when I ran into a snowstorm between Watson Lake and Whitehorse. I had come all the way from Wisconsin with very little sleep. Between being really tired and not making any time anyway, because of the poor visibility, I decided to pull over and take a nap at one of the many turnouts. I just put a pillow against the window and pulled a sleeping bag over me.

I awoke from the cold about three hours later. It was still dark and the windows were all frosted up, so I started the truck and turned the heater and lights on. By now I'm fully awake and I realize I don't know which way to go! Did I pull off on the left or right side of the highway? I had been so tired I couldn't remember. I got out of the truck to look at my tire tracks, but they were gone, blown shut by the shifting snow. So I'm wandering around away from the truck, trying to find a track, when I finally gave up. When I looked back towards the headlights, I could barely make out the faint parallel lines of my tire tracks coming off the highway. From then on, every time I stopped to sleep, I parked the vehicle in the direction I needed to keep going.

* * * * * * *

The first real hint that my dog-racing career was coming to an end was the afternoon I got home from work too late to train two teams. It seemed like beating someone with a dog team was becoming less and less important. Instead of quitting early enough to train two teams, which I should have done, I had decided to train one big team of twenty-two dogs, the ones that absolutely had to be exercised. It was the biggest string I had ever put together, so I left the yard with a little apprehension, dragging a small tire to help with the control. The trail that afternoon was down the river, a trail I never got tired of running. The dogs liked it too because there were no hills or sharp corners to break up their rhythm.

I liked running the river because of the intimate stories I got to relive as the team loped by. Just a few bends below the house is where my dad shot his very first deer. He took it right at the base of the ear, with a .22 rifle, in the summer time. A mile below there is the spruce tree where cousin Lance nearly caved in my head with a rock, by accident of course. Downriver from there, just below his house, we had cleared a downhill ski trail from the top of the highest hill around, down onto the river ice. Lance's claim to fame came when he skied down that hill with his broken right leg in a full cast, and made it!

Practically every 100 yards I could relate a story, like just above The Forks where the tractor tipped over, pinning Mom's leg under the rear tire. They had been going to gather some wild honey that day. Down below where the Indians used to camp is where Brian Edinger and I caught up with a wounded buck late one evening in hunting season. The deer died in the middle of the river, so I stripped to my shorts, walked barefoot out on the shelf ice till it broke, then waded in thigh deep water to drag him in. It only hurts for about fifteen seconds before everything goes numb!

The sixteen-mile training run that evening was long enough to go beyond the places I was familiar with. I had heard of Red Man's Eddy and Shaw's Eddy, but I didn't know them as I went by. Finally my trail split and I hollered, "haw" as the leaders took the left hand fork. It angled over tight to the south bank before making a sweeping arc across the river ice to the north bank, where we turned upstream and headed for home, reconnecting with the outbound trail. The dogs naturally jumped into their harness a little harder now, they were always eager to go home.

Before we got back to familiar country, there was an extra pretty little stretch of river. Clinging to a steep slope on the right hand side is a delightful grove of hemlock and white pine, as the river bends to the left. Against this background, my leaders swept into the curve and they and the next three pair behind them were so far ahead that I could watch them run from the side, their quick, fluid, efficient strides in unison with each other and in rhythm with the team. The twilight of the setting sun was at just the right angle, so I could see every puff of their breath as it hung in the still air, added to by each succeeding pair. The only sounds were the panting of the dogs and the barely audible whisper of the runners.

It was the most beautiful moment I'd ever experienced behind a dog team and I slipped into the romance of the moment, a man alone with his dog team in the wilderness of an icebound winter. For a brief moment I fell back into the fantasy of my youth and imagined myself a Jack London character in a desperate race to reach my trapline cabin before darkness gave the trailing wolf pack the courage to close in. This was why I had gotten into dogs in the first place. I had come a long way from my original dreams.

It was funny how much I'd changed over the many years of racing dogs. In the beginning I hated training, wishing it was race day every day. At the end, I loved training, watching the young dogs develop into top athletes. I had started to resent the traveling, restaurant food and sleeping in strange beds. There finally came the afternoon in January of 1991, when I had to force myself to quit logging, so I could load up the dogs and head for the Ely race. I knew then it was time to quit.

I remembered when Dick Brunk told me he was getting out of dogs and my incredulous response: "How can you? You're exactly what I'm trying to be, and now you're just walking away?" He just kind of smiled and said, "Aw, all the fun was getting there." At the time I could not understand. Now I did. All the fun had been getting there, looking forward to next year, knowing things would be even better. But winning had not been as wonderful as I had expected. I still had to work like a dog all summer to make ends meet. Perhaps I was finally experiencing burnout. Whatever it was, I was finally forced to face the fact that I didn't enjoy it anymore and I knew I was incapable of doing it just for recreation. If I wasn't giving it my all, where would the satisfaction come from? To this day, I have this reoccurring nightmare of showing up at a dog race knowing that the team is totally unprepared. I always wake up really disgusted with myself.

Quitting was very hard. Dog racing had defined who I was, the guy with the dogs. I sold most of the dogs after the '92 season, but kept the young dogs and some breeding stock just in case. Two years later, when I knew for sure the fire in me was not coming back, I sold everything.

Would I do it all again? You bet! I had gained a more worldly education and had found that Kennan wasn't such a bad place to live after all. Leanne and I had witnessed some unforgettable sights, like the night the Northern Lights put on a most glorious display while we were on our way up the Alcan, just north of Whitehorse. That night the entire sky was filled with the shimmering, haunting sheets of red and green and white. It's the sort of thing you have to see to believe and only made possible from our involvement with dogs.

I had met some very unique and even famous people. There was Peter Norberg, a top dog musher from Tuktoyaktuk, a village to the east of where the Mackenzie River runs into the Arctic Ocean in northwest Canada. He was one-half Eskimo, one-fourth Indian, and one-fourth Swede and had lived the kind of life I enjoyed reading about. I never tired of his stories of running a trapline with a dog team and hunting caribou and polar bear. Then there was Dick Moulton, an old time dog musher from New Hampshire, who had been with Admiral Byrd on his third Antarctic expedition. Dick was one of the few dog mushers I looked up to; not only for being a good dog man, but also for the way he conducted himself on and off the track. He was a real gentleman.

But if you asked who was the most famous person I'd met, I would have to call it a draw between the Vice-President of the United States, soon to become President and one of the greatest baseball players to ever play the game. It all happened on the same day, with a few more VIPs thrown in for good measure.

In 1988 I returned to Laconia, New Hampshire, to defend the world championship crown. Race weekend fell just before the very important Tuesday of the New Hampshire presidential primary. They have a joke out there during primary season that whenever you find three people on a street corner, you will find a politician. It's darn near true!

I was by my dog truck on Saturday, well before race time, just fiddling around, when one of the race organizers came quickly up to me and said, "Come on Gary, there's someone I want you to meet." Jean Bryar was a tall, slim, very attractive gal who had been the top female dog trainer and racer in the '60's and '70's and was the only musher to ever appear on the Johnny Carson Show. She grabbed me by the arm and hustled me clean across the parking lot, like I was one of her dogs. We had to hustle because this little group we were trying to catch was moving away from us. As we were gaining on them I spotted a fancy, long, black, mink trimmed ladies glove lying on the snow, so I scooped it up, figuring it belonged to someone in the bunch ahead. When we got close enough, Jean said in a loud voice, "Michael, Michael, there's someone I'd like you to meet."

So this little swarm of people stops and turns around and suddenly I am face to face with Michael Dukakis, who went on to become the

Democratic nominee for President. I also noticed Kitty, his wife, missing a glove. Jean said, "This is Gary Edinger from Wisconsin, our defending World Champion." I had the glove in my right hand, so I tucked it under my arm, so I could shake his hand. As we were shaking hands I felt Kitty, who was behind me now, retrieve her glove. I was so focused on Mr. Dukakis, I didn't turn around, to try to explain how I had come to have her glove. Mr. Dukakis asked me a few questions about dog racing and listened intently as I answered. At the end, he told me his handlers had him on a tight schedule and he had to get going, like he wanted to stay longer and had to apologize for not being able to. As he walked away I thought, "What a nice man." That's probably why he didn't win the Presidency.

A few hours later I'm getting dogs out to start harnessing for the race when Jean comes hustling up to me again, "Come on, there's someone else I want you to meet." When I hesitated because I thought I had better things to do right then, she said, "It'll only take a minute," and grabs my arm and hauls me off again, like I didn't even have a choice!

This time we didn't have to go very far and this time there is a really big crowd. With me in tow, Jean just plowed right through there, like a polite moose wading through alders, "excuse me, excuse me" and when we hit the center, here's George Bush Sr., the current Vice President of the United States! Jean just walks up to him too and also, like they are on a first name basis says, "George, I'd like you to meet our defending World Champion, Gary Edinger from Wisconsin."

As we shook hands, the Vice President too asked me a question, only this time, while I'm answering, he's not paying any attention to what I'm saying, just smiling and waving at people in the crowd around us. For a brief moment I thought "how rude" and toyed with adding, "and your mother wears army boots," but caught myself in time. It turned out that Mr. Bush didn't have much charisma, but he was probably one of the most qualified Presidents we ever had.

Right when we finished, there was a commotion off to my right and into our little circle rolls this short, really fat guy, with a big man following him. The fat guy turns out to be the New Hampshire Governor, John Sununu, and he has a surprise guest for the Vice President, major league baseball's great Ted Williams! "Wow, no wonder this guy hit so many home runs," I thought. He's big and even at his age; you can still see the power this baseball legend had. Somehow I got introduced to him too and after shaking his hand asked, "What in the world are you doing hanging around with politicians?" (I know, you don't have to tell me, it was a stupid thing to ask.) He answered matter of factly, "Oh, I think George is a good man. I'd like to see him get elected." I wanted to ask him for his autograph, the people back in Kennan would never believe this, but I couldn't bring myself to do it. Those guys get pestered so bad. As I walked away I thought, "Boy, what Grandpa wouldn't have given to have been standing there next to me!"

To cap the whole thing off, Congressman Richard Gephardt, another Democratic candidate, showed up and shook all the open racers hands as we were lined up for a photo, before the start of the race. I was surprised how small he was; he looked bigger on TV. He was real muscular and fit, about my size, perfect for a dog racer. I commented to him as he got to me, "You'd make one heck of a dog musher, too bad you're wasting away as a politician." He thought it was funny too.

I had a horrible race that day, but in the end it all evened out with a story I'll be able to tell my grandkids about the time I was introduced to a man who a short time later became the President of the United States.

With my involvement in dog racing, I had found out more about myself than I otherwise would have. Doing it the hard way has given me a tremendous sense of accomplishment. I had found the Edinger pride, perseverance and tenacity was strong enough to overcome the many obstacles, setbacks and disappointments along the way. It was similar to chasing Larry around on snowshoes or packing heavy moose quarters out of the woods. You just have to keep putting one foot in front of the other, only this time I had done it for nineteen years. With sixteen dogs on the line and something going haywire, I'd learned to think fast, on my feet, under pressure, and to go with my gut instincts. That training would later play a huge role in saving my life. Lastly, I'd found I had married a really good woman, pound for pound as tough as my mom. Without her, I never would have pulled half of this off.

Leanne and her Silver Medal Seven-Dog Team.

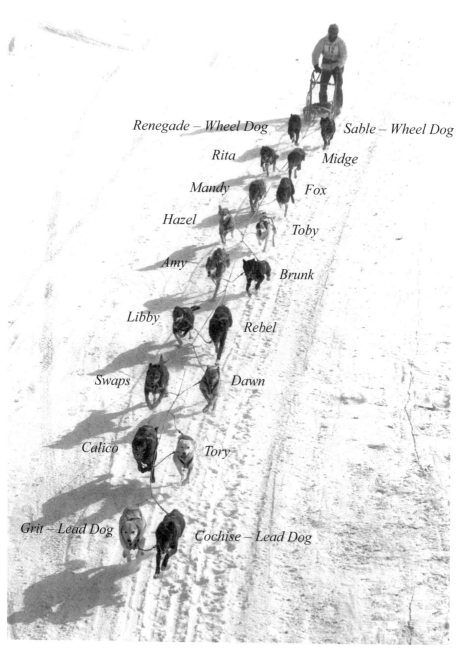

Renegade – Wheel Dog   Sable – Wheel Dog

Rita   Midge

Mandy   Fox

Hazel

Toby

Amy

Brunk

Libby

Rebel

Swaps   Dawn

Calico   Tory

Grit – Lead Dog   Cochise – Lead Dog

First day of the Fairbanks, Alaska, race in 1986.

Chapter 8

THE YUKON

A man came running out of the woods wearing one of those fancy outfits piano players wear, a black top hat and tuxedo with long tails in the back. I slammed on the brakes of the pulp truck so I wouldn't run him over and I was jolted back to reality.

It was early in January of 1980, about 3:00 in the morning and I was easing my way out of the woods with my second load, having been up all night. I hadn't really fallen asleep; I was just hallucinating. There is a difference.

Dick Brunk, a musher from Alaska, had showed up sort of unexpectedly on Monday evening to stay with us for a few weeks. While on the road, it's common for dog drivers to stay with other local mushers, using their training trails and hospitality between race weekends. I'd invited Dick to stay with us after the Ashland, Wisconsin, race, but he had said he didn't know what he was doing yet. It had snowed all day Monday, while I was working, so after supper that night, I took the snowmobile and broke out the trail on the river, knowing Dick would want to train his two teams the next day. I had hit several small patches of overflow, which can cut the dogs' feet when it freezes. I figured if I worked all night, I would have time to fix the trail Tuesday morning before Dick needed to train. That's why I saw a piano player come running out of the woods.

During the summer, Dick built log cabins around Fairbanks, where he lived. At the end of his stay with us that January he said, almost as a passing comment, "If you ever need a job, give me a call. I'll put you to work." I'm not sure what inspired him to say that. Perhaps he liked the workmanship on my own log house or he thought I was a good worker.

That comment stuck in my head, so two years later, in April of '82, I gave him a call. Logging was going into one of its normal bust cycles and it looked like I was going to need some summer work. Dick said, "Sure come on up. I'll pay you $12 an hour," which was well over what I made driving truck.

I had a one-ton truck for hauling dogs, so I took the dog boxes off, but left the sleeper on, right behind the cab. Another dog musher friend, Ted Roeder, a professor at the University of Stevens Point, needed a ride for a student who had a summer job in Alaska. I willingly agreed to take him along. With both of us driving, we would make good time.

The first part of June, I gave Leanne a good long kiss and told her I would see her in forty-five days. She was going to fly up, halfway through the summer, for a week. Since our first date, we had never been apart for more than a week and we both knew this was going to be hard.

My first trip up the Alcan felt like a real adventure. At Dawson Creek, we stopped and took a picture of mile 0 of the Alaska Highway. It wasn't long before we could see snow-capped mountains off to the west, but it wasn't until we had gone through Fort Nelson that we got into them. The scenery was everything I thought it would be, and the road was as rough as others had predicted. After passing beautiful Muncho Lake, we stopped to visit the Liard Hot Springs, a natural sulphur springs which is nearly 100 degrees where it comes out of the ground. Back at the truck, I told the young fella he could take us the 135 miles into Watson Lake while I crawled into the sleeper for some much needed sleep.

I was sound asleep, in the wee hours of the morning, when suddenly the truck pitched hard to the right. Gravel was pinging off the underside and limbs were banging against the cab. My young driver had fallen asleep and driven off the road on the passenger's side. He was now wide-awake, like me, and fighting to keep the driver's side tires on the road. I hollered, "Hang onto 'er!" and he floored the 454 motor, hauled the wheel back hard to the left and we spun our way back up onto the roadbed. Of all the places to drive off the Alcan, he had found one of the better spots. There were plenty of places where you would not get a second chance. I never asked him to drive after that.

With a minor cracked windshield, we cruised on up the highway. We made a quick loop through the fabled town of Whitehorse and on up past the barren, almost moonscape of Kluane Lake. At Beaver Creek, we crossed into Alaska and 300 miles later; I dropped my traveling partner off in Fairbanks.

Dick lived at a place called Thirty Mile, which was thirty miles southwest of town along the Richardson Highway. It was a dog mushing community of about ten dog drivers who had built a common training trail, which they all used in the winter. After finding Dick's place along the Tanana River, he showed me my headquarters for the summer, a little twelve by eighteen log cabin. It didn't have running water, but it did have electricity.

My first job was cutting and peeling a set of house logs on Dick's land. He put an ad in the paper, and what was left over, I sold as firewood. I went over to a neighbor gal, Kathy Christman, to get her to skid everything out of the woods with her workhorse one day and the funniest thing happened. She had a visiting neighbor who, when he heard my name said, "Hey, I know you! You're that guy that won Bemidji in the five-dog class back in 1972." I was shocked! Who in the hell would know such a thing? Richard Barnes, originally from Minnesota, had also been in his first race then and he remembered me. His house was the next place down from where I was staying and we ended up becoming good friends.

Of the limited number of white people I got to know in Alaska, Kathy Christman was the only one who had actually been born there. Everyone else had come from "outside", (the Lower Forty-eight). From what I could tell, most of them had left their homes to escape the stifling confinement of their upbringing, as well as for the adventure. Although I found everyone pleasant and welcoming, there was not the sense of community I was used to. No one cared what you did in your private life, as long as it didn't bother them.

Our first cabin to erect was up on Chena Hot Springs Road. I had used the butt and pass method to build my home, so Brunk had to teach me how to make saddle notches, where you cut a cup out of the log above, to fit over the one below. We used the chinkless method to fit

Chainsaw carpentry – making a saddle notch in Alaska.

the logs together by simply passing the chainsaw bar back and forth 'till the logs fit tight together. I know chainsaw carpentry sounds pretty crude, but I got pretty good at scribing and fitting the logs for an airtight fit.

Dick only worked five days a week, so I used weekends to work on the house logs and the firewood. I knew Leanne had her hands full keeping things going at home and I would have felt guilty taking any time off. I was in Alaska to make money.

The middle of July finally arrived and I can still feel my arms wrapping around Leanne's skinny waist at the Fairbanks Airport. The excitement to be back together again was unbelievable. Dick gave me some time off, so we could have time together and I could show Leanne some sights. Kathy Christman offered to take us up to the Yukon River. She said the trip along the Trans Alaska Pipeline, on what everyone called the Haul Road, was very scenic. Kathy also thought it would be fun, when we reached the river, to use her canoe and motor on downstream to visit dog mushing legend George Attla at his summer fish camp. What Hank Aaron is to baseball, George Attla is to dog racing. When I had won my first race in the five-dog class, George had won in the Open. We had bumped into each other several times since then and I certainly knew who he was and he kind of knew who I was. Kathy knew him really well.

Fish camp is a place where fishermen go to live on the banks of a river for the summer to fish the annual salmon runs. Most of the camps are for subsistence use, smoking and canning salmon for winter food as well as drying fish, late in the season, for dog food. George also had a commercial permit, which allowed him to sell the fish for hard cash. Commercial was highly regulated. The only way to get a permit was to buy one from someone who wanted to sell, for whatever price both parties could agree upon.

There were two ways to catch salmon on this stretch of river. You could use a set gill net in an eddy or you could use a fish-wheel. George had a permit for both, so he took us on a tour of the operation, where we watched him pick fish out of his net and unload them from the holding box of his fish-wheel. I was instantly enamored with his fish-wheel. It's a kind of stationary water wheel, powered by the current, which scoops the salmon up, as they are swimming upstream. Legend has it that it was invented in China and I thought it was a really neat contraption. George said he had made some real good money fishing the last few years. It looked like a great way to make a living.

Leanne's visit came to an end much too soon. Letting her go was extremely difficult. As I watched her jet disappear into the twilight of the midnight sun, I vowed never to do that again.

We finished the house on Chena Hot Springs and then started on one next to where I was staying. Dick subdivided a small parcel from his land and we put up a two-story house, which he would later sell. He hired another neighbor, Dale Raitto, who was a little younger than I was, to help with the upper story.

At first glance, Dale can come across as a pretty macho guy, but when you get to know him, as I did, you'll find he's an intelligent, kindhearted person. Don't get me wrong, you would find it easier to go around than over him; he's just macho in a good sort of way. We became really good friends and he would become a strong part of my Alaskan story in the coming years.

I was supposed to leave for home after the second house was finished, but Brunk took a job re-roofing his ex-wife's house in town. Somehow he conned me into staying an extra seven days. I needed to get home to start fall training, but more than anything else, I wanted to see my honey. After work the last day, Brunk tried talking me into a good night's sleep before heading out, but I was in a real hurry. I wanted to see Leanne really bad. I called her to tell her I was getting ready to leave. She knew me well enough to remind me to, "Drive careful."

I had agreed to haul a couple of young dogs down to Jim Harvey, a good open class musher who lived just south of Edmonton. It was close to midnight before I was packed and ready to hit the road. Despite working hard all day, I had no trouble staying awake. The highway was much smoother than it had been in the spring and I made good time all that night and all the next day. On marathon trips like this, the first twenty-four hours are the worst. After that, you just kind of get numb.

The following night I'd made it well past Watson Lake before I had to start using my tricks to stay awake. I can't take No-Doz or caffeinated drinks because caffeine really upsets my stomach. My tricks include turning up the radio/tape player and singing as loud as I can. Rolling the window down and sticking my head out and letting the cold air lash my face works pretty well too. My last trick, when all else fails, is to stop and get out and run around the truck three or four times as fast as I can. That night my tricks didn't last too long. It began to feel like my steering arm was detached from the rest of my body, doing a great job, while my mind wandered into a fog. Finally, I began to hallucinate. Out of the corner of my right eye, I could see Dick sitting over on the passenger's side and he wanted me to stop and nail a two-by-four in the middle of the road! I tried to shake it by running around the truck, but it wasn't long before he was back, telling me once again to nail that board in the road. After the third time, I somehow realized I'd found my mental limit. At the next turnout, just before Muncho Lake, I pulled over and crawled in the sleeper. In the few seconds before I fell asleep, I realized I knew more about myself. I had found my max, and in some twisted way, a sense of accomplishment came with it.

For some unexplainable reason, I woke up two hours later feeling rather perky. I let the two dogs out of their crates and gave them a drink of water, then jumped behind the wheel and continued on, just as daylight was waking up the mountain peaks around me.

I hurried through Fort Nelson, Fort St. John, Dawson Creek, and Grand Prairie, stopping only when I needed gas or to drop the dogs. Don Cousins, a musher I had just gotten to know, lived right on the highway, just before Valleyview, Alberta. I swung into his place to feed the dogs and say hi. His wife, Faye, said she was going to have supper ready soon and I was welcome to stay. I was getting pretty hungry, so I gladly accepted.

Don tried to get me to spend the night. A good night's sleep in a comfortable bed was mighty appealing, but this sense of competition of how fast I could make it home, was beginning to take hold. I reluctantly declined, and headed south once more.

An hour and a half later, I was kicking myself for not staying, because I got really drowsy. A good meal can do that to a person. I found a little wayside and crawled into the sleeper, just as the sun was setting.

Just like the night before, I woke up two hours later; feeling refreshed enough to keep going. At the first town I came to, I called Jim Harvey to get directions to his place. I told him I would get there before daylight, but he said that was okay. The barking of his dogs would let him know I'd arrived.

I had a difficult time following Jim's directions when I got close to his place. I knew I was close, so I kept trying different roads for almost two hours until, right at daylight, I spotted all his dog houses behind his house, next to a little barn. We unloaded my two passengers into his dog yard and I was treated to a good breakfast of bacon and eggs. Looking at a map, Jim helped me figure out the best way home from his place. It looked like crossing the border at Portal, North Dakota, was the best way to go. I was anxious to get going; I could almost smell Wisconsin from here!

In the middle of that afternoon, I pulled over for a quick nap again, and just like the other two times, woke up after a solid two hours sleep. Well after dark, without any hassle from the border guards, I crossed back into the United States. It was a crystal clear night with a big full moon, perfect for traveling. It seemed like every song on the radio was one of my favorites and I was on a natural high. I stopped at 2:00 in the morning in a little town called Bowbells, North Dakota, and called Leanne from a phone booth. After I heard a sleepy "Hello" on the other end, I said, "I bet you won't believe where I am!" I figured to be home around noon and asked her to call in sick, so she would be there when I pulled in. She couldn't bring herself to do that, but that didn't dampen my eagerness to continue this race against myself.

The stretch between Fargo and St. Cloud was a real struggle, because of the monotonous freeway driving, but I managed to stay awake. Eighty-six hours after leaving Fairbanks I turned into my driveway. Counting the time from when I'd woke up, the morning before I left, I'd been going 104 hours, four and a third days straight, on a total of six hours sleep. What a trip!

* * * * *

Brunk's heart had not been into building cabins that summer. He had gotten out of dogs a year before my arrival and he hadn't figured out what to do with the rest of his life yet. Dick was one of those guys who was looking for a happiness unobtainable to humans. We had gotten along well all summer, but I could see he just didn't know how to be happy. Dick called me that December and asked if I would be interested in buying his fish-wheel permit for the upper Yukon, the same section of river Kathy, Leanne and I had visited that summer. He had traded three acres of land for the permit, thinking that might interest him, but now he just wanted to travel, to sell his ties to Alaska. He said he wanted $12,000 for the permit, which was $3,000 less than the going rate at the time.

Of course I had to think about it, but not for long. A chance to really do this gripped me, the same as the excitement to begin racing sled dogs had. The bank said they would loan me the money, as long as I put up everything I owned for collateral. A few weeks later, I called Dick back and told him I'd take it.

We had a pretty good winter racing dogs. I won the International Sled Dog Racing Association's gold medal in the open class and Leanne won the silver medal in the seven-dog. As soon as race season was over, I started getting organized for fish camp. I bought an eighty-five-horse outboard motor to power the twenty-foot johnboat Kathy Christman said I could rent from her. Leanne organized a leave of absence from her clinic job and sent resumes off to all the medical facilities in Fairbanks. A young gal from Phillips, Penny Albiniak, agreed to take care of the dogs and house sit for the summer. I ripped out the little propane cook stove from my old trailer house, gathered up a wall tent, small barrel stove, and other camping supplies along with a tight, strong, nylon mesh material to build a smoke-house. My new Alaskan friend, Dale Raitto, said we could use his place, out at Thirty Mile, for our base of operations. I built a tow bar for Leanne's little Ford Pinto, hooked it to the back of the one-ton, and headed for Alaska once again, for the summer.

I didn't know a thing about catching salmon with a fish-wheel. Someone suggested that I should go see George Attla, the champion musher who we had visited at his fish camp the summer before. Perhaps he would be willing to help me out. Word had gotten out in the mushing/salmon fishing community that a new guy was going to be on the river, so my visit came as no surprise to George. One of the first things he said, with a calculating eye, was that my truck would make a darn good fish hauler. When I suggested that if he would teach me how to fish, there might be a way for me to help him back, Attla was receptive to the idea. He said he was going to build a new fish-wheel and if I helped him build his, then he would help me with mine. He also was going to build a new log home later on and I could help him with that, knowing I had worked with Brunk the year before.

The first run of king salmon would arrive at the bridge towards the end of June, so we had about three weeks to get ready. (The Yukon Bridge is the only one in the state to span the river, built to support the pipeline and the oil development on the North Slope.) I made a list of the materials George said I would need for the wheel: an 8x8 for the axle, some 2x6s, nails, cabin spikes, a long cable, heavy wire and a roll of wire mesh, a little heavier than chicken wire. Following Attla's instructions, Dale helped me get the poles ready for the baskets. We selected some young spruce poles, about the size of my forearm at the base and peeled the bark off, except for the last five feet. The bark was left on so that, when we heated the tips over a campfire, the wood fiber was steamed inside the bark. Then the poles could be bent over a frame in the right shape and allowed to dry. Dale was a really big help because he had seen enough wheels to know what things should look like. He even went along with George and I a few times to set up George's camp. It was interesting and exciting to him, too.

Alaska's interior had been home to Athabascan Indians for centuries. Although the state had just settled the Native Land Claims Act and the area I would be fishing was mostly public land, I completely understood the sensitivity of the locals to a white man, an outsider no less, barging into their area. Although Attla was an Athabascan, he too was not a local, having been raised on the Koyukuk River, farther to the west.

In the area of the bridge, the elder I would have to get permission from was Charles "Tucky" Mayo. Shortly after my arrival, George took me down to Tucky's camp one evening to see where it would be all right for me to put my wheel and fish camp. George told me to let him do the talking.

Tucky owned the land where his camp was and he had a nice little cabin there. Although he now had a place in Fairbanks, he spent most of his time on the river, fishing in summer and running a trap line in winter. When George introduced me as being from Wisconsin, Tucky asked if I knew where Janesville was. He said that was where his grandfather was from; a Swede who, during the gold rush days, had floated down the Mackenzie River in Canada and portaged over to the Porcupine. He floated down the Porcupine into this stretch of the Yukon and married a native woman. I think that gave me a little "in" because I was from the land of his grandfather. The other thing that helped my case was that I was a dog musher. Dog racing is to Alaskan Natives as baseball is to most American men. George didn't come right out and ask where I could put my wheel and camp, he phrased it as, "Do you think it would be a good spot?" That would give Tucky a polite way out, if he didn't want me there. Tucky pointed out that the water was pretty fast where I was thinking about putting my fish-wheel and the bank was pretty high where I wanted to put my camp, but he thought they "might be all right." I had his permission.

The spot for my camp was about nine miles below the bridge, on the north bank, in-between George's and Tucky's camp. There was a very tiny stream there for fresh water and although the bank was steep and high, there was a fairly flat place on top, for my wall tent and smokehouse. From my camp, I could see the spot far upstream and across the river, where my fish-wheel would be. The current was faster there, because a small river entered the Yukon from the other side, building a gravel bar out from its mouth, narrowing the mighty river there. No one had tried to put a wheel in this spot because it would be harder to hold everything in the swifter current. From watching the way fish swam upriver in the spring at home, I knew by placing the wheel at the head of the small eddy along the bank, it would be a natural spot for the fish to funnel

91

through.

Back in Fairbanks, I mounted the motor on the back of Kathy's twenty-foot johnboat and built a console, out of plywood, for the steering wheel and controls. Dale gave me a bucket seat from an old, stripped down Volkswagen he used as a dog training cart, which I bungee corded onto the bench seat at the back of the boat. The tall back on that seat was going to save me from an awful lot of grief the following year.

Headed up to the Yukon with the boat and poles for the fish-wheel.

Prospects for a job at the hospital looked promising for Leanne, but there were no openings yet, so she came with me to set up my camp and to build the wheels. We built a very comfortable home for the summer by first laying a plywood floor on small log stringers, leveled across some good-sized blocks of wood. On top of that, we built a frame of poles for the wall tent, adding an extension in the front for the kitchen, which we covered with clear plastic sheeting. I used a heavy piece of plywood for a door, crafting hinges from 4x4s and using a couple of cabin spikes for hinge pins. I built the smokehouse about eight by eight feet, by digging four corner posts in the ground, tall enough so it would accommodate two layers of drying racks. I put a roof on it and wrapped the sides with the heavy nylon mesh material I'd brought along. For a smoker, I simply laid a fifty-five-gallon barrel on its side and used the loose cover to regulate the airflow.

To build the fish-wheels, George and I first gathered together a bunch of dry driftwood logs to build the rafts, on which the fish-wheels would spin. As he floated the logs into place, four on the outside, where the fish box would be, and three on the side that would be next to shore, I spiked them into place. In the center, we built up a bracket, one on each side, to hold the axle. Onto the axle we attached the two pre-built baskets, one opposite the other, and then attached one of the paddles on top, opposite the baskets.

George then tied his boat onto the whole thing and pushed it over to where it was going to do its work. We tied the raft to a big tree on the bank way upstream with a long cable. We then attached a long, small diameter log to the front of the raft, called the spar log, and pushed the wheel out into the river, anchoring the butt on the bank, after finding the right depth. When the wheel was spinning, you wanted it to barely miss the bottom. Then we spun the wheel half a turn, so we could attach the other paddle. The paddles helped power the wheel when both baskets were out of the water at the same time. You regulated the rate of spin by adding or subtracting boards on the paddles. The wheel was supposed to spin pretty slow, only about three RPM and when you wanted to turn it off, you just put a pole across the raft at the front, stopping a basket as it came down.

You build a raft and then add an axle.

Baskets attached to the fish-wheel.

Only one thing remained. We had to put in a lead, a fence made of peeled poles, which blocked the fish from passing between the wheel and the bank. A boom log was placed from the center of the raft, angling back down

My fish-wheel in place, ready to go.

river to the shore. From that the leads were sunk, using ropes to hold them down to the bottom.

So here's how the whole thing worked. As a salmon was swimming upstream it would bump into the lead (fish barrier), angling out

93

Leanne standing on my fish-wheel.

Building my tent camp.

towards the wheel and deeper water. As the fish cleared the end of the lead, a basket would scoop it up and before it could escape, was lifted out of the water. As the basket was lifting in the air, the fish would be thrashing around, so it slid down into a chute, which angled out the side of the wheel. Before the basket reached its vertical height, the salmon had already fallen out the side, into the holding box. To unload the fish, you simply pulled up on the outside of the raft, even with the fish box and tied up. From there you transferred the salmon into the boat by hand. I always figured it worked so well because the river was so dirty. The silt ran so heavy in summer that when you put your hand in the water, up to your knuckles, you couldn't see your fingertips!

I really liked the twenty-four hours of summer daylight. The bridge was just below the Arctic Circle, so the sun would set at midnight, but just barely. The daylight gave me plenty of energy and if you got tired, you could go take a nap at any time. There was plenty of opportunity to get your work done. The camps operated on '"river time" which meant they ate breakfast around noon and supper after midnight, when commercial was closed. They all thought I was a hard worker, because I was always up and at 'em by 8:00.

Leanne was with me when I caught my first fish. I had just turned the wheel on that night and was drifting away, when I thought I saw a fish tail flop into the box. Sure enough, I'd caught my first king. By the end of the forty-eight-hour period, I'd caught about ten, averaging about twenty-five pounds apiece. We took them back to town, where I already had a few orders for fresh Yukon kings, and sold them for $1.50 a pound. Leanne had a job waiting for her, so I headed back up on the 140-mile, three-hour trip to fish camp alone, to begin fishing in earnest.

In my stretch of river, the season was divided into two forty-eight-hour periods per week. The first was from Friday at 6:00 p.m. to Sunday at 6:00 p.m., closed for forty-eight-hours and re-opening Tuesday at 6:00 p.m. till Thursday at 6:00 p.m. The closure was to allow for enough

My first king salmon.

escapement to the spawning grounds. A guideline harvest range (quota) was set before each season, based on how strong the Commercial Fisheries Division, of the Alaska Dept. of Fish and Game, thought the run was. You had to report your catch at the end of each period. When the harvest guideline was met, the season was closed. It was the fisherman's responsibility to listen to a program called "Trapline Chatter" on Fairbanks radio station KJNP, where the closure of season would be announced.

The basic life cycle of king salmon is easy to explain. After the eggs hatch into small fry, they make their way down the rivers and out into the ocean. They swim around out there for six or seven years, growing ever bigger, before the urge to spawn overwhelms them. Somehow (scientists think by smell) they find their way back to the very stream they were born in, some swimming 2,000 miles to the headwaters of the Yukon, where they spawn and die.

Mixed in with the fully mature salmon during the run are a fair number of three- and four-year-olds we called jacks. Because the jacks were only about fourteen to twenty pounds, half the size of the big ones, most of the commercial fisherman didn't sell them because the quota would be filled too quickly. Instead, the jacks were filleted and cut into strips to be smoked, right at fish camp, some of it for personal use and some was sold later, mostly to friends. Fish strips are the most delicious thing I've ever tasted.

I was told that normally there would be a fish buyer at the bridge, but

George came back from town one evening with the bad news that there would be no buyer for the kings. Attla turned out to be a pretty good businessman. He had found a good market for our fish in Anchorage at $1.50 a pound live weight. We would just have to get them there. That's where my good fish hauling truck came in. At the end of each fishing period, he would buy fish from others at seventy-five cents a pound. I would make the first run to Anchorage, which was 500 miles away. With the loading and unloading the round trip would take a good twenty-four hours, so George hired a young fella named Chuck Kokrine to help me drive. He too, was from a dog mushing family. George would turn my wheel on for me on Friday evening, because I would not quite be back yet.

Getting ice to ice down the kings on the Fourth of July.

George would take the second load down, after fishing closed on Sunday, with his one-ton. We would haul each other's fish for free and I would get fifty percent of the profit on my load for hauling the other people's fish. I was told this was how it was going to be. Attla didn't ask for any input, but I thought the profit margin was pretty high. By now I had gotten to know another fisherman and dog musher, Freddie Mayo. He was Tucky's nephew and his camp was just across from George's. It didn't seem a very fair way to treat friends. I guess that's why I'm a crummy businessman.

When George went to pay me for my first run to Anchorage, he said I was making too much and cut me back from fifty to twenty-five percent. I just let it go. There were other little things that Attla had shared with me which made me feel that, although he was a great dog musher, perhaps he wasn't someone I wanted to be associated with.

George told me about the time he had purposely gone out of his way to anger another champion musher, over a dog deal, for no other reason than to beat him in a dog race. Attla hoped the other musher's personal anger toward him would give George some kind of an advantage while they were competing on the trails.

COLOR SECTION

The accident scene in the Wisconsin woods where I almost lost my life. Note the bloodstain on the stump at lower center. Points of interest include:

   1 – Clump I ended up sitting astraddle of.
   2 – Stump my left leg was trying to clear when the tree hit.
   3 – The tree that kicked sideways and sheared my left leg off.
   4 – Where the accident started.
   5 – Small, hung-up leaner that kicked the tree sideways.

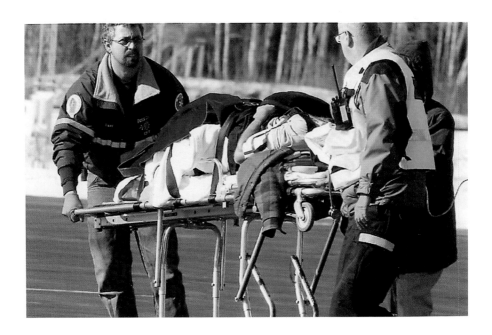

The two photographs on this page are of the ambulance crew that literally saved my life. I'm shown above after being placed on the stretcher and just before I was loaded in the helicopter in the photo below. Photos courtesy The Phillips Bee.

Gary in front of his pole skidder.

This is a "barber-chaired tree" that stayed on the stump.

The ambulance crew that saved my life. Left to right: Jim Cejka, Dave Chamberlain, Gary, Bryan Curtis, Mike Tyrrell, April 2007. My accident gave them impetus to get approval to do IVs.

"Reserved parking" sign in the woods for a handicapped logger, set there as a light-hearted tribute to Gary's insistence that he would return to logging. Set-up and photo by Bill Hendl

Putting my leg on at the trailhead, 2008.

Leanne standing on my fish wheel.

My brothers and sisters. Back row from left, Kay, Me, Peggy and Jerry. Front row, from left, Carol, Nancy, Betty, and Larry.

Leanne, me and Garret in 1987.

Aubrey and me on a spring canoe trip.

Garret and me with our year's furs.

Me with Garret in the sled.

Receiving my International Sled Dog Racing Association Gold Medal with Leanne in 1983.

Leaving the starting chute in Fairbanks, Alaska. Photo courtesy the Fairbanks Daily News-Miner.

Leanne and team on the second day of a race at Green Bay, Wisconsin.

Talking about sled dog racing to Medford seventh graders.

Garret, me and Aubrey, and Leanne ready to leave the trailhead into the Bitterroot Mountains, 2001.

What a view!

Aubrey and Leanne. We started taking Aubrey to the mountains when she was three.

Eating lunch in the Selway-Bitterroot Mountains, about 1995.

The view from the top is incredible. Big Creek Lakes, Selway-Bitterroot Wilderness.

Gary with his packstring in the Bitterroot Mounntains in 2008, the year after his accident.

Me and pack mules on our summer trip in 2009.

109

A nice bull I got in 2006, a year before my accident.

Packing out my elk on our 2006 hunt.

Me, at left, and Larry carry moose quarters on our hunt in 1971.

Me and Larry and a small bull moose I killed on our hunt in 1972.

"My family hunting crew – cousins and nephews. Back row, from left, Moose Edinger, brother Larry, Tom Henderson, Me, Tanner Edinger, Tim Henderson, Dale Timmers, Brian Edinger and Dave Edinger. Front Row, from left, Travis Edinger, Troy Henderson, Jess Edinger, Kenny Moore and Josh Edinger.

"The Legacy" – I had this painting done by artist Kelly Meredith, inspired by the visit from Great-Grandpa (See Chapter 5 for story). It's him, Grandpa and my Dad in the background and Garret carrying the guns, including the old .32, and, of course me with the buck in the foreground.

Another incident had happened just a few years before, which was a real eye opener. According to Attla, he had been fishing a big eddy, just below the bridge on the south side, every year. Some white guy came along and tried to horn in on him. Although legal, first-come first-serve every year, it was very unethical, much the same as putting your deer stand where someone else has hunted for years. They had words over the dispute, neither one would back down, so they both ended up having a gill net in the eddy.

George said he was suddenly catching very little and suspected the other guy of stealing fish out of his net. He waited, concealed, up on the bank one day with his .308 rifle. Sure enough, he said he caught the culprit red-handed, so as the fisherman was leaning over the side of the boat, picking another fish out of George's net, Attla fired next to his head, into the water. The guy started hollering and waving his arms like crazy. George worked another shell into the chamber and this time put the sights right on the thief, thinking, "The hell with this, just kill him." He decided not to, but as he finished the story, he looked me in the eye and said, "You know, it would be easy to kill a man," and laughed. My goal was to just get through the season on good terms and next year, keep separate from him.

I had a good king season. My wheel was the best producer in the neighborhood. Because so few guys were able to sell fish commercially, we never did reach the harvest guideline, so we got to fish the entire run, which lasted about a month. Then there was a break of about three weeks before the commercial fall chum season would start. There was going to be a buyer at the bridge, which was a really good thing because there was no way for us to keep up hauling chums. For my wheel, a good day for kings was about thirty fish, while a good day for chums was over 300. Just to show you the difference in numbers, the harvest guideline for my stretch of river that year was 3,600 for kings and 43,000 for chums. Chums, which were also put up for dog food late in the season, only averaged seven pounds and we would receive around $2.00 per fish at the landing.

First, I got busy repairing my wheel and leads. Joints, poles and wire mesh had worked loose and had to be repaired. I hauled extra fifty-five-gallon drums of gas to camp because, when the fish were running heavy, I'd be running the boat pretty steady. Dale got a subsistence permit and we arranged for him to come up, before commercial started and catch a bunch of fish for dog food for him.

George came down to camp one evening, about a week after kings were done and said he was going into town to start on his house. I told him I'd be in as soon as I could, knowing it would take George a while before he had the foundation and floor joists laid, so we could start setting logs. I should have known better.

Once, while I was at George's camp, Freddie Mayo had come over, we thought to visit. During the conversation, Fred mentioned that his chainsaw was broke. After he left, it dawned on George that Freddie had wanted to borrow his saw, so George threw his saw in his boat and ran it over to him. It was that polite, old native way of asking for help that I totally missed.

It was a week later, after I was done helping Dale catch his dog food, when I ran into town to start helping George. As I was walking up to the construction site, it looked like my timing was perfect because he was in the process of laying the last of the floor joists. Boy was I wrong! Attla just tore into me. "Where have you been? I needed your help last week putting in this foundation! I treated you better than I treated my own son and this is the thanks I get! I don't need you; I don't want you around! Get outta here!"

My mind was reeling as I walked back to my truck and started to drive away. I thought maybe I could reason with him, so I turned around and went back. "George, I'm sorry I didn't come in right away. I wanted to get ready for chum season and I promised Dale I'd help him catch some fish. You have all the logs to lay, which I am good at. Here I am. Put me to work." But he was having none of it. My plan of parting on good terms at the end of the season hadn't worked.

I felt really bad about it. Without me asking him to, Dale tried to plead my case a few days later, but Attla wouldn't change his mind. Dale tried to ease my conscience by telling me George had plenty of help and the whole thing was probably contrived to run me off, now that he didn't need my fish hauling truck anymore. I'm sure Attla felt a little heat from some of the other fishermen for bringing an outsider on the river, but that wasn't fair. I would have been there, with or without George. Even Freddie tried to make me feel better. He had a way of looking at everything in a humorous way. "We all had bets as to how long you and George could be partners," he said in a laughing voice. "You made it longer than just about anyone else ever has. No one can stay partners with George." Perhaps George saw me as a future threat on the dog racing trails and wanted to get under my skin, like that other musher he had told me about. Whatever his reasons, it was done and I could not fix it. Like so many other things in life, I wasn't going to get a second chance to get it right.

Commercial chum season finally started. I saved out some fish for smoking and by the end of season the smokehouse was full again. As soon as season closed, Leanne quit her job at the hospital and came up to help me break camp. I saved my fish-wheel for next year by clearing a place high up the bank, so the ice wouldn't take it out the next spring. After I took the bottom paddle off, I laid poles down as skids and pulled the wheel way up the steep bank by hand, using a come-a-long. It took all day. After I tallied up my summer earnings, I had made some pretty good money, but I hadn't gotten rich, like I had hoped.

That winter, while we were racing dogs, I started hearing about threats Attla was making against me. He was telling others, "He better not come back," or "He won't have many friends," and "He won't be welcome." The most serious one I heard was while I was at the Fort McMurray race. A Canadian friend of George's told me Attla had said to him, "If Gary comes back to the river, that'll be the end of him!" This guy added, "I think he meant it. If I was you, I wouldn't go back."

I felt threatened, all right. Having that story Attla had planted in my head about nearly killing that other guy was very unsettling. But it would take more than threats to force my obstinate Edinger pride into surrender. It's not that I'm really that brave, I just don't know how to back down.

Leanne couldn't get another leave of absence, so she was staying home. As I was leaving for Alaska, I can still see her in the rear view mirror hunched over, hugging her waist, crying; fearing what might await her stubborn husband. As I wrote this, I asked her how come she didn't try to talk me out of it. She got this incredulous look on her face and said, "That would have worked? No!"

On the way up, I stopped to help someone with pickup trouble just north of Haines Junction. The old Chevy pickup had its hood up and another guy had already stopped to help. I, of course, had my toolbox along, so I pulled in too. (It's an unwritten rule to stop and help those in need on the Alcan.) It was a young Indian from New Mexico, going up to work near Anchorage. His parents were along to help him drive. When I saw that the rotor wasn't spinning under the distributor cap, when he turned the motor over, I knew it was something that couldn't be fixed without parts. I towed them the fifty miles into Destruction Bay, alongside Kluane Lake, where there was a phone and services. That was the best I could do for them. I felt a kinship with the young Indian. Like me, he was headed for Alaska on an adventure, trying to find something better, but sometimes running up against more trouble than we bargained for.

I got to the Yukon a little early that year. The river was still really high from breakup, so I caught drift logs for the fish-wheel raft as they were floating by. There was a little message for me when I went to slide my wheel down onto the raft. An empty cigarette pack, the brand George smoked, lay perfectly centered below my wheel on the ground.

Although everyone said you couldn't put a wheel in by yourself, I managed to do it. It seems to me there's always a way. Instead of someone holding the other end, I used a bungee cord or tacked it with a nail. In place of human strength, I used a come-a-long. Sure, it was the hard way to do it. My friends from Thirty Mile would have gladly helped; I just wanted to see if I could do it. Later, when Dale found out what I had done, he laughed at me and said, "God damn, when someone tells you you can't do something, you just have to prove them a liar, don't you." He laughed because we both knew he was the same way.

A day after I had finished putting my wheel in, I was putting the finishing touches on when Attla roared up in his boat. Without a "Hi," or "How do you do," he snapped, "I want my cable back!" in an angry voice. I must have given him a confused look because he followed with, "You borrowed some cable from me last year and I want it back!" Oh yes; now I remembered. I hadn't brought enough cable to anchor my wheel to the bank last year and George had offered to lend me some of his for the season. Instead, Dale had given me some that he had laying around. When that's what I told him, he gave his wife a scowling look, like her memory was off, she shrugged her shoulders, and he went roaring off. I had been working on setting my wheel for a week, but he had waited until it was all in place, before confronting me, planning on making me re-do a lot of the work. He checked out my story, but Dale's memory was as good as mine.

Attla was set up to be the big time king salmon buyer at the bridge that year, but of course, he wasn't going to be buying any of my fish. Lucky for me, Freddie Mayo had an acquaintance who wanted to buy a limited number of kings, about as many as Freddie and I could produce. Our buyer, Wade, supplied us with some real nice insulated fish totes, which were going to figure into a really bad accident, later that year.

116

This Wade guy turned out to be one crazy sucker. After the first commercial period, I rode into Fairbanks with him to help him clean the fish and buy some supplies. I should have known something was up when Freddie, seeing us off, said to me, "Have a safe trip," and laughed.

The Yukon River is a half-mile wide at that spot. The landing and a little truck stop are on the north end of the bridge, which slopes uphill to clear the south bank. By the time we reached the south end of the bridge, we were doing ninety MPH. and he maintained that speed, as close as he could, all the way to town. Much of the Haul Road was cut into the sides of real old mountains and it was so wash- boarded that I normally kept the speedometer on forty-five. We went chattering around those curves almost sideways sometimes, with hundreds of feet down on one side or the other and no guardrails. I knew it would be useless to protest, so I just hunkered down on the passengers' side, trying to act unconcerned, all the while hoping Wade would be capable of winning the Baja 500 and we wouldn't blow a tire or meet another vehicle at just the wrong moment.

We finally cruised onto the blacktop just outside of town. Wade looked over at me, slapped me on the shoulder and said, "You're all right. Most guys would have claw marks in the dash by now!" I just smiled.

It turned out Wade had a partner in town. He was a younger white guy and I got the strongest feeling that there was something crooked about him; like this fish buying was just a cover for something else. I never saw any proof of that; it was just a feeling. All three of us got the fish cleaned that night and the next morning Wade wanted me to meet a guy down in Nenana, so we jumped in his truck again. I figured he had driven like an idiot the day before, just to get a raise out of me, but nope, he always drove like an idiot! At least the trip down to Nenana was only half as dangerous because it was all paved.

We visited with an older native named Edmond Lord, who, I was told, was a very important man in that town. On the way back to Fairbanks, Wade shared with me that Edmond thought I was all right. Whatever test I had been put to that morning, apparently I had passed.

Before leaving town for the river that evening, Wade picked up another passenger he knew, that needed a ride to the bridge. The young native had killed a guy in a drunken knife fight and because the judge felt it had been partly in self-defense, the young man had spent the past six months in a halfway house, trying to get him pointed in the right direction. Sadly, when we picked him up, the young fella was already

117

drunk. Wade had been smoking pot all afternoon, (it was legal in Alaska) and it mellowed him out so well that it proved to be the only time he was safe to ride with! On the leisurely drive back to the bridge that evening, I had plenty of time to reflect about the characters I had gotten myself tangled up with this time. I figured the wise thing to do was to keep them at arms length as much as possible. I often wonder if Wade is still alive. I seriously doubt it.

I found that every year I was on the river, I would get "bushy – my term for turning into a recluse. By the time the middle of July arrived, I went into town only when I absolutely had to and then, tried to time it for 2:00 or 3:00 in the morning, when hardly anyone was around. It was always such a relief to get back out of town, like it was easier to breathe. I've never liked dealing with lots of people for very long. It takes too much energy.

George's prediction that I would have no friends turned out to be just the opposite. Besides Freddie, I'd gotten to know Bill Roberts, whose camp was about a mile below the bridge. He told me that, although he was half white, the white people would have nothing to do with him, while he was growing up, so he was raised in the native customs and culture. You could not find nicer people than the older natives like Bill and Tucky. I enjoyed listening to their stories about trapping with a dog team, the threatening wolves during the hardest winters, cutting wood for the steamboats that used to run the Yukon, and the colorful characters they had known, some left over from the gold rush days.

Tucky was the one who told me the best hunting story I've ever heard. It went like this…

There was this guy from Stevens Village (upstream from the bridge) who had something to do downstream one early fall day. In those days, and even when I was there, the natives used smaller boats and motors, usually fourteen footers with a twenty to thirty-five horse on the back. He took along his .35 Remington pump rifle, just in case he spotted a moose. As luck would have it, he did spot a nice bull moose swimming across the river later that morning. Moose are totally helpless in the water. Normally, a guy would pull alongside the animal and plug it behind the ear, then tow the carcass to shore, where he would butcher it. Well, on this day, the subsistence hunter had a great idea. He tied his boat to the bulls' horns, and turned off the motor, letting the moose do all the work. He got so lost in daydreaming about how he was going to tell his story, to show the people back at the village what a crafty man he was, that he totally lost track of time and place. Suddenly, the moose was gaining the bank and our crafty hunter went to belatedly pump a shell into the chamber, but the gun jammed! He barely had time to jump out, gun in hand, as the boat disappeared, chasing after the bull up into the timber. He heard quite a commotion for about 100 yards, as the poor little boat ricocheted off trees, before there was a final wumph! He got his knife out and pried the jammed shell loose, then went to track his boat down. He first found the motor, with part of the back of the boat still in its grasp. Presently, he found his craft, all beat to hell, wedged between two trees, with the moose and tie up rope long gone. He did become famous, but it wasn't for being crafty.

Attla started doing little pesty things, like going past my camp close to shore, wide open, so my boat would slam around against the shore. Normally a person would slow down or swing wide around another fisherman's camp. One day, while I was in my tent, I could hear a boat motor upriver being gunned then being cut, gunned then cut. I went out to the shore to see what was going on and there was George, gunning his boat up past my fish-wheel, then drifting down, gunning up past my wheel, then drifting down. He did that for about forty-five minutes before finally going back upriver. The next day he was back and did the same thing. This went on for four or five days. I figured he was trying to get under my skin, so I just ignored it. A few days later he beached his boat below my wheel and was walking around on the bank. I went and got my .30-06 rifle, so I could look through the scope to see what he was doing. As he drifted away from shore, it looked like he was putting out a gill net. Sure enough, when I went up to empty the fish box that evening, there was a net in the little eddy, just below my wheel.

Rifles were common in fish camps. Although grizzlies were not common in that area anymore, black bears were thick, and cutting and smoking fish had a way of attracting them. Although I never had a bear in camp, Bill Roberts had to kill two or three every year. That was the only way to get rid of them. Tucky had managed to snare one that year, which had been raiding both of our fish-boxes. Even Freddie's wife, Annie, would carry a bear rifle when she went blueberry picking. She was as comfortable packing that rifle as most women are carrying their purse!

I started carrying my rifle with me in the boat after Attla put the net below my wheel. I thought perhaps he would claim I was stealing fish out of his net and take a potshot at me, the same as he had the other

119

guy. Every time I pulled up to my wheel, I would scan the lightly-wooded bank for possible danger.

George lost some respect from our neighbors for trying to cut my wheel off with his net. Tucky said to me, "Gee whiz, I can't believe George would do that to a man." Annie thought it was too bad that I wasn't an Indian. She said I would probably get drunk some night and cut his net loose! Lucky for me, the net seemed to have no effect, because I kept catching kings at about the same rate. After three fishing periods, Attla picked up the net.

I'm sure many people will think this all sounds like the Wild West. Well, it was! Just a few years before I started fishing, a criminal was trying to hide along this stretch of river. He made the locals mad because he raided one of their camps. A fisherman spotted him walking along the bank, a few days later, and so, pretending to be friendly, approached the thief with an offer for a ride. When he got close enough, the fisherman picked his shotgun up from the bottom of the boat and made a citizen's arrest at gunpoint.

The year before, I had bumped into the State Troopers a couple of times, putting their boat in at the landing to go upriver and investigate some pot-shots at recreational fishermen on the Dall River. It was a popular place for military personnel from Fairbanks to fish for big northerns. The investigations were just a formality because, when questioned, the locals all had the same answer, they didn't know anything. The message was clear though; outsiders weren't welcome.

In May of 1983, just before I started fishing, a shoot-out had occurred over in Manley Hot Springs, not far from where I was. Some nutcase, originally from Illinois, had driven to the little end of the road community on the Tanana River, below Fairbanks, and camped along the river for almost a week. For some reason, he went off the deep end and killed everyone that showed up at the boat landing one afternoon. By the time the whole thing was over, nine people, including a State Trooper, were dead. They finally gunned the killer down from two helicopters a few days later.

About a week after the net incident with George, I was just finishing the supper dishes when I heard a boat coming into my landing. When I looked out the door, here was George's boat just swinging in. I had had enough. There was only one reason for Attla to be coming into my camp. I knew he was looking for trouble and I intended to give it right back. I grabbed my rifle, rammed a shell in the chamber, and stepped out on my little porch to wait for the son-of-a-bitch.

I caught little flicks of movement between the brush and trees, as I followed his progress coming up my trail. As he drew near, I brought the rifle up and pushed the safety off. If he had a gun in his hand when he came around the corner of the smokehouse, I was going to let him have it! To my great relief, around the corner came Chuck Kokrine, the young fella who had helped me haul fish to Anchorage the year before. He had borrowed George's boat to come down and visit me. As he stepped up onto my little porch he asked, "What's the gun for?" I calmly replied, "I thought you were George," my response belying the flood of relief I was feeling. Chuck had been studying me closely and my response only gave him a slight pause. He simply gave a little nod. We went in and had a nice visit.

Either Chuck said something to Attla or it was mere coincidence, but that was the end of George's harassment. Attla had been right. It would be easy to kill a man.

*　*　*　*　*　*

For us river people, it was common for everyone to give complete strangers a lift, either by boat or by truck. It was just another form of public transportation. As long as you had room, it would have been an insult to say no. Early during chum season that year, I was making my last run of the day, timing it so that I could just make it back to camp before dark. This particular evening, there was a young native couple with a newborn waiting at the landing. I was just getting ready to fasten down the cover of the fish tote, after finishing unloading my fish, when they came up and asked if I would give them a ride down to Pitka's camp, about two miles downstream at the narrows. I took it real slow going down. The wind coming upriver had whipped up the waves pretty good that evening and it would have been a rough ride for the young gal and the new baby she was holding in her arms.

After a "Thank you very much" and a "Glad I could help," I once again swung downstream. I was behind schedule now and it was getting pretty dark, so I rammed the speed control wide open. An empty twenty-foot boat with an eighty-five-horse motor strapped on the back can really move. The boat was just getting up on step, when I decided to stand up, so that I could better see any drift running in the river, reflecting off the surface in the twilight. Just as I reached cruising speed, WHAM #*#, the lights went out!

When I came to, I was slumped back in the drivers' chair. The front of my raincoat was covered with blood and the boat was headed back upstream. (If I would let go of the steering wheel, the boat would naturally turn to the right.) I pulled the lever back to idle. I could see blood running off the end of my nose pretty good, so I put my hand to the bridge of my nose, realizing then that my glasses were gone. When I pulled my hand away, it was covered with blood, so I wiped it off and felt my forehead. My hand came away clean from there. Using my fingertips, I found the gash between my eyebrows. My vision is pretty bad without glasses, so I started feeling around the bottom of the boat, trying to find them. When I got near the fish tote, ahead of the console, I saw what had happened. Right when I was going to fasten the cover down was when the young couple had asked for a ride and I had forgotten all about it. It was the cover that had flown up and hit me square between the eyes, knocking me out and my glasses in the river. I would have ended up in the drink too, had it not been for the high back of Dale's Volkswagen seat. Who knows what would have happened if I had ended up in the river. I always wore my lifejacket, so I wouldn't have drowned, but the circling boat might have run me over and it certainly would have piled into the bank or a rock at some point. If I would've had to swim to shore, the current would have taken me far downstream, by the time I made the bank. Holding direct pressure on the gash with my left hand, I eased down to Freddie's camp.

I figured Annie would patch me up, but she wasn't there as I walked into Freddie's tent. Fred's eyes were pretty wide as he asked, "What happened to you?" I couldn't resist. "George and I had it out. You should see what he looks like!" I only let the look of horror last on Fred's face for a few seconds before I said, "Naw, a cover from one of Wade's fish totes flew up and hit me in the head. Can you patch me up?" As he worked on me, sitting by his table, nausea started coming several times and I had to put my head down by my knees to control it.

With tissues stuffed up my nose and a butterfly type bandage on my forehead, Fred got the bleeding stopped. He volunteered to run me up to my truck so I could get my spare pair of glasses, even though it was dark. Back at Freddie's camp, he wanted to follow me down to my camp to make sure I made it, but I figured I was all right. It was just hard to concentrate for very long.

About 10:00 o'clock the next morning, when Freddie walked into my tent to check on me, I wasn't feeling so good and was still in bed. He took one look at me, laughed and said, "You look like hell!" I started stirring around later that afternoon, and when I looked in a mirror, I did look like hell. Both eyes had turned black and blue and I had those blood stained tissues sticking out of my nose. I could take care of myself all right, but it was two days before the fog left my head and three weeks before my eyes returned to normal. For a long time afterwards, every time I heard the hard acceleration of the truck or boat motor, I had this almost uncontrollable urge to duck!

Fred turned out to be a darn good friend on the river. We could count on each other for help at anytime. Towards the end of chum season, one evening, I was headed back to camp and noticed a bunch of boats at Freddie's. He had just gotten a brand new, custom-made boat, with a 150-horse motor on the back. Maybe they all wanted to check out Fred's boat, like me. When I entered his tent, I knew I had made a mistake. They had clearly been drinking for quite a while and the stares I got were not very welcoming. When I said, "No thanks," to an offered beer, someone said, "What's the matter. White guy too good to drink with us?" Then they started in, God-damning white guys.

Freddie didn't let it go too long before he jumped in. "Gary is my friend. He's not like them; he's more like us. He's a good guy." Someone responded, "There's millions of good guys in the world. We going to let them all in here?" I told Fred I'd come back tomorrow, for a ride in his boat, and eased my way out of there.

The next day, while Fred was showing off his boat to me, he said, "I meant what I said last night. You are a good guy and you are my friend, but if you ever bring another one up here, that will be the end of our friendship." I told him I understood because I would feel the same way. At home, when I take someone to a favored fishing or hunting spot, that courtesy of friendship does not extend to their friends and sometimes I explain that, just as Freddie was doing now. As far as the racism was concerned, although I resented it, I understood it. The natives had plenty of good reasons not to like white guys.

The following year, 1985, was my last on the river. It looked like my hopes of making some real money just wasn't there and it was hard for me to justify being away from Leanne that long. Kathy Christman had sold her boat, so I bought a used one in Fairbanks. That year, we had a buyer from Fargo, North Dakota, for our kings at the bridge. George was way down at the mouth, buying fish down there.

Dale's construction business was a little slow, so he came up and spent a little time with me on the river, obviously liking it there. One day

I asked him if he would be interested in buying me out. Everyone on this stretch of river knew and liked Dale, even George. I knew he would fit in well. I'd sell him everything; permit, camp, fish-wheel, boat and motor, for what I had in it after king season, and I would help him fish the chum run. He said that sounded like a good deal. I worked it out with the fish buyer so that I would drive home after kings were done and could catch a ride with him from Fargo, when he flew his small plane back up for chums.

One evening, as I finished dropping off my kings at the landing, a white lady, about my age, asked me how far downriver I was going. She had a little scarring on her face, I guessed from an old burn, but she was not unattractive. She was well spoken and presented herself well, but a glance at her clothes told me she had fallen on hard times. She wasn't even carrying a pack, like a traveling person normally would. She explained that she, "just had to get to Nome" and had heard that the barge, which was tied up just above the bridge, was going there. She had hitchhiked from town to the bridge, in hopes of hiring on as a cook or something, but the captain had told her no. I explained that taking her nine miles down river would be of little help and any idea of hitchhiking by boat all the way down the Yukon and then up the coast to Nome, was not very feasible. When I left, she was just sitting on the beach.

The next morning, as I approached the landing with my morning load of kings, there was a strange lump on the beach. Just before my bow touched shore, the lump moved, as the lady from the night before, threw off the wool jacket she was using as a blanket and uncoiled herself from a little nest she had dug among the rocks. It was cold, right around freezing, and when I told her I couldn't believe she had slept like that, she said it wasn't that bad. She'd found that if she put her head under the coat, her breath helped keep her warm. It was a trick I remembered from my youth; trying to stay warm in my own bed, on those cold winter nights.

A tidal wave of guilt washed over me. I could have easily invited her down to camp for the night. I had a spare bed, a warm tent and plenty of food. This poor gal. But then I thought, "That's the last thing you need; to wake up in the middle of the night with some crazy lady standing over you with a butcher knife!" But still...

I had figured she would get a room at the truck stop for the night, but now I fully realized how bad off this lady really was. "When's the last time you had a good meal?" I asked. "It's been a few days." I pulled out

124

my wallet and handed her a $10 bill. "Here, go and get yourself a good breakfast." I was short of cash myself right then, having borrowed $200 from Dale to tide me over until money from the kings started coming in, but she obviously needed it more than I did.

She took the money without a fuss, but then she wanted to buy me a cup of coffee. When I explained my dislike of coffee, she insisted I should have a cup of hot chocolate then. It's pretty funny that she wanted to treat me with my own money, but she seemed desperate to show her thanks, and that was the only possible way she had. I finally gave in.

I expected her to order a big, logger style breakfast, but all she ordered was a roll and a cup of coffee. As we visited, I wanted to ask her what was so important in Nome, but it was none of my business. Back in Kennan, I would have asked for her entire family history, but Alaska is such a different place. After she paid the bill, she stuffed the $6 and change in her pants pocket; for a rainy day I suppose. She said she was going back to town and wash dishes, until she had enough money for a plane ticket to Nome. I told her that sounded like a good plan, shook her hand, and wished her luck. I read her as a good person, deserving of help, who had perhaps married wrong or made one bad decision. It's funny isn't it, how such a brief encounter can create such a lasting memory. I often wonder how her life turned out and if the meager $10 I gave her made a difference.

The world I found, when I got away from Kennan, was often not such a wonderful place. At home there was this safety net, a comfort zone, of family and community that you knew would help you if you ever really needed it. It was hard for me to imagine the desperation the lady who had to get to Nome must have felt and how alone she must have been. That's probably why she insisted that I accept a cup of hot chocolate: to have some company, if only for a little while, to be near someone who actually cared. I reveled in being alone on a landscape where self-reliance was a necessity, but I was lost in a crowded world where the only way out was a credit card. What a contradiction that is! As much as anything else, my traveling showed me that, as bad or as tough as you might think you have it now, if you bother to look around and notice, there is always someone else who has it worse. It's almost embarrassing to take comfort in that.

After a fairly short king season, I drove home and spent a good three weeks with Leanne, before I had to drive up to Fargo for the return trip to Alaska. The fish buyer had a Cessna 185, a four seater, which he was

125

going to use to fly fish from the surrounding villages, once we returned to the bridge. It was a fun trip. What a great way to travel. We made it all the way past Watson Lake, that first day, and landed at a little place called Teslin, British Columbia, for the night.

The next morning we were fogged in until about 10 o'clock, when the fog finally lifted enough so we could fly. I had left a message for Dale on the radio program "Trapline Chatter" that we were on our way, so when we reached the Yukon later that afternoon, we buzzed Dale at fish camp, on our way to land on the Haul Road. Not long after we had gotten out of the plane, Dale was there to pick us up. I had made it from home to the Yukon Bridge in about forty hours, with a good night's sleep included. It sure beat driving!

It was a strong chum run that fall. The buyer put Dale and me to work helping to ice down and load fish into the refrigeration vans, when we weren't tending our own wheel. After hauling and throwing fish on the last day of season, I changed into a cleaner set of clothes, out of my duffle bag, and Dale hauled me into the Fairbanks Airport. Once inside, he went one way and I went the other, asking the airline agents if they had anything leaving soon, so that I could get to Fargo. Dale hollered from the other end and motioned me down. The ticket gal said she had a flight leaving in a half hour for Anchorage, with a connecting flight to Seattle. There would be a two-hour layover before I could board a plane to Minneapolis with a connecting hop to Fargo. A travel agent could not have planned it any better. I never gave a thought to how I might smell or look or for that matter, the good-sized folding knife I always carried on my belt. I was headed home.

Saying goodbye to Dale wasn't too hard because I knew I'd be back up there racing dogs soon; if not this year, then next. He had been a great help and a true friend. There has only been a couple of other guys who I have enjoyed being around that much. Thanks to Dale, Freddie, and Richard Barnes, (another Thirty Miler I mentioned before) I could count on Alaskan help anytime I needed it. Bill and Tucky had helped keep the loneliness at bay. They were all really good people.

The airports at Fairbanks, Anchorage, and Seattle were much the same in that there were a lot of working class, normal looking people walking around, wearing everyday clothes. Many had backpacks and hiking shoes on, my kind of people. When I stepped off the plane in Minneapolis, what a culture shock that was. Everyone was dressed like they were going to a wedding, while I had on my everyday clothes and work shoes that still had Yukon River dust and salmon slime on them. I felt really self-conscious. Even worse than that was when they took my knife away from me. I'd flown into those other big cities, no problem, but I couldn't fly to little Fargo with it? At first I thought they were kidding. The lady said the captain would have it for me in a sealed bag when I deboarded at Fargo, but I wasn't to open it until I was out of the airport.

And so came an end to my career as a commercial salmon fisherman. It had been a real adventure where I had pushed myself to my own mental limit and where I had found the limit I could be pushed by others. Going forward, my main focus was still on developing a top dog team but I needed to fill in with a job that made good money and allowed me the freedom I had come to enjoy. I decided to buy my own logging skidder and become an independent logger. I knew it was a hard way to make a living, but I was no stranger to that. I already had some sawdust in my veins and logging held everything I was looking for.

Chapter 9

WESTERN MOUNTAINS AND WILDERNESS

After I got sled dog racing and salmon fishing out of my system, I settled down in Kennan. Well, sort of. My brother-in-law, Tom Henderson, had died in 1981 from a blood clot caused by a stomach aneurysm. My sister Betty, left with a house full of kids and a farm, hung on for a while, but finally fell in love again and remarried, selling the farm in Kennan and moving to Phillips. Tom had liked to hunt as much as the Edingers and my family had absorbed him into our tribe. In this setting, it was natural for his sons to want to carry on their famiy's heritage. The fourth oldest boy, who was named after his dad, came to live with Leanne and me during his senior year. The hunting was better and easier around my house, plus his two older brothers, Tim and Thad, lived just down river, keeping that land in the family.

Young Tommy was a lot like me when I was his age. He had turned away from the things most young men are interested in, like drinking and fast cars, and he was the happiest when he was outdoors. After high school, Tommy went out West to guide school and at the young age of twenty-two, started his own outfitting business in the Selway-Bitterroot Wilderness of Montana and Idaho. With such a handy connection like that, it wasn't long before I was going out every fall guiding elk hunters for Tom and doing some elk hunting of my own.

Since I had more time at home now, I also got more involved in community issues. My first project was to try and keep the elementary school in Kennan open. Studies had proven that the closing of their school was the number one reason for the death of small communities. Wisconsin had passed a school funding formula that quickly started squeezing rural school districts like mine economically. With a group of other concerned parents and community leaders, we managed to hold off the inevitable for almost ten years, but money, not education, finally won out. Public education is what made America great and Wisconsin had one of the best systems. Currently, the way we pay for education in this state is starving our educational system.

I also found my footing on environmental issues; much of my new views being shaped by my travels racing dogs and guiding. In Alaska, I had experienced real wilderness. When I started going out West, the places I went to were designated wilderness, set aside by government, with rules and regulations to protect them. It became crystal clear to me that the key to having quality hunting opportunities was to restrict motorized access. Because our homes were adjacent to a large block of county forest, a very small group of us started pestering the county forest administrator to put stricter regulations on ATVs. Like most government agencies, we could not get them to act until the off road damage to the resource became a crisis. After twelve years of working on it, we were forced into a compromise, setting aside 8,000 acres in a long skinny block as a limited motorized access area and the forestry committee having the authority to gate other areas, if excessive damage continued.

While I was working on motorized access to public land, I also helped form the Friends of the Jump River, created to protect the natural pristine qualities of the river us founding members owned land along. Between things going right in logging, dog racing, and the price of land, I had added to the family eighty acres with four more forty-acre pieces, the whole works connecting into one irregular block. The river ran through every new forty and we bought them, not as an investment, but as a way to protect the river and our peace and quiet. I had purposely built my home so it could not be seen from the river, not wanting to ruin the natural river corridor. In 2004, our group received the "River Champions Award" from the River Alliance of Wisconsin. I was chosen to give the acceptance speech near the Capital building in Madison. The setting was close and personal as I gave the speech that night, speaking from notes, but mostly from the heart. That night I was definitely singing to the choir…

On behalf of all the members of the Friends of the Jump River, I'd like to thank the River Alliance for this award. We think this is a really big deal and we're honored to have been chosen. (Cathy Mauer and Gordy Ruesh, from Medford, were standing behind me, along with Leanne, for moral support) There really are more than four of us. (Laughter) There are eight. (More laughter) Well, a few more than that. But we are a very small group. We've managed to puff ourselves up by being involved in other conservation/environmental groups in the area. Each of us seems to be involved, as individuals, elsewhere and every time they get publicity, Friends of the Jump River also seems to get mentioned.

Our president, Dan Haupert, who's mostly responsible for us receiving this award, couldn't make it tonight. At our last meeting, he asked for a pretty face to put on a suit and come down to say a few words. After he lowered his standards, I said I'd give it a shot. (Laughter. I wasn't wearing a suit either.)

According to some of my neighbors, you are looking at a bonafide, in the flesh, environmental radical! (Eruption of loud applause) The irony here is that I'm a logger! (Laughter) So now, in order to fit into my new image, I introduce myself as a tree-hugging logger. (Loud laughter)

I'm the fourth generation to own our land along the river. My great-grandparents came to the banks of the Jump in a covered wagon from western Iowa in 1903. That river is where my dad took me fishing, where I hunted grouse along its banks, where I trapped mink and muskrats in the fall so I could buy some decent school clothes, where us kids swam after a hot July day of making hay and where we ice-skated in the winter. In short, the river was like a magnet, always drawing me to her. It didn't matter if I planned to do something south of the house when I stepped out the door; it wasn't long before I was headed north towards the river. Everything happens along the river. Once during a summer flood when I was six-years-old, she gave serious thought to drowning me, but for reasons known only to a river, spit me back out. Maybe she knew that someday I would become a voice, to advocate keeping her wild and free. That she knew her beauty and serenity and soft whispering on a warm summer night wouldn't be enough for some. That some would say we could improve upon that.

How many of you know where the Jump River is? (About half raised their hands) Oh! Quite a few! Well, do me a favor and let's keep it a secret. (Laughter)

All four of us founding members own land along the river. We formed to protect its natural, pristine character. It's a simple concept and we thought it would be easy. What's so hard about keeping something just the way it is! All you have to do is leave it alone! And yet, I'm finding it's easier to get public and political support to fix something after it's wrecked than to protect and preserve it before it gets there. Why do we continue to spend all this energy wrecking nature just so we can spend more energy to try to fix her again? It seems a trait unique to the white man.

All of us who care about natural resources are having a hard time right now, what with a state legislature that wants to ruin it all and

130

a President who could care less. Part of the problem is in us. Quiet recreational activities attract quiet people. The last place we want to be is in a crowded, noisy, public hearing room with angry faces staring back at us from the other side. We have to keep showing up and try to get our neighbors, who believe as we do, to come along. We have to keep trying!

In closing, I'd like to leave you with a thought from Aldo Leopold. I couldn't find the exact quote so I'm going to have to paraphrase. It went something like this, "Gauge yourself not on the goals you achieve, but gauge yourself on how hard you try!" The real test is in the trying! Thank you.

The crowd rose to its feet in a standing ovation. As I turned to leave the podium, Leanne said, "You really outdid yourself this time!" I wasn't aware that our Lt. Governor, Barbara Lawton, was in the audience. Among many others, she sought me out afterwards and said that it was one of the better speeches she had heard, especially the part about having to wreck things just so that we can restore them. It was all pretty heady stuff.

In 1999 the Wisconsin state legislature passed a law requiring all counties to develop a comprehensive plan to show "how and where new growth should be accommodated." I eagerly accepted a position on our county grass roots committee, representing the logging/forestry industry. From my travels, I had seen what was happening in other rural areas of the nation and I was pretty sure those changes were headed into my community. Specifically, I was worried about the effects of tourism. One of the things I had my eye on, when I decided to come back to Kennan, was all those tourists streaming up from the south every weekend. The main travel corridors of Highways 51 and 53 were sucking everyone into the beautiful sandy lake areas of Hayward and Minocqua. I figured no one would want this mud and mosquito country in the middle, and I would be safe here. Boy, was I wrong. Once those places filled up, there was no place to spill over but here.

Tourism is said to be very important to the economy of many states. From my travels, it looked to me like it was very important to a few business owners, but the wages it pays are mostly for entry level jobs or part time work. My views were reinforced when I attended two separate rural economic development forums. The experts all agreed that jobs that you could raise a family on and would hold your young people in your community do not come from tourism. In short, a local economy based on tourism will ensure that the working class will remain poor.

The price of land in rural areas was traditionally set by what the land could produce. When I was growing up, cleared farmland had more value than forest land. For a long time, wild land value was set by the simple method of being able to cut enough timber on the property to pay the taxes. In all my travels, this part of northern Wisconsin had the cheapest land anywhere. No one wanted it. As the upper Midwest became more affluent, that all changed.

As outsiders began to gleefully pay up to ten times more for land than it was worth, locals began to gleefully take their money, not thinking or caring what might be left for their kids or their neighbor's kids who might want to stay. Of course, the taxes increased dramatically too, forcing many into selling land they couldn't hang onto anymore, even if they wanted to. Old families who had worked so hard to build their communities were now being forced from the choicest properties, forced to live on ever-smaller tracts of land. The wooded properties became the most valuable, bought for hunting land, and "hunting shacks" began springing up like mushrooms on a warm summer day. The new owners didn't like being alone, so they started bringing their buddies, who started spilling out onto the public land, crowding local families who had hunted that country for generations. Confrontations developed, even between resident neighbors, because everyone was being squeezed. It became more difficult to have a quality hunt or to find a buck with a decent set of horns. The peace and quiet of rural living became rarer every year.

I saw this Smart Growth law as a chance to address a lot of these issues. One thing in particular I wanted to do was to identify our unique natural features and develop a plan to protect them, long term. Some saw this all as a power grab to infringe on their personal property rights. Their self-reliant individualism, which is present in most rural people, wouldn't allow community rights, or the rights of the next generation to enjoy what we all had enjoyed, to trump their personal rights. Although my committee was successful in getting a state grant to pay for half the cost of creating a plan, the personal property rights group hollered loud enough to persuade the county board to give it back. To date, we don't have a plan to guide the future of our county. We never even got to sit down in a room and discuss what we might want it to look like.

The battles over ATV access and Smart Growth made me mentally tougher. Country people are very sensitive about their reputation. The insults, name-calling and lies being hurled around, trying to discredit the messenger, made me very defensive and bitter at first. I finally realized that the people who really knew me and what I stood for, plus the ones who were willing to investigate the issues on their own, were the ones that mattered. To hell with the rest of 'em! Once I figured that out, life got easier.

In the late 1990s, while elk hunting, another door opened up. Tommy's business had grown so much, that he didn't have time to hunt with his uncle anymore. He could spare a day to help me backpack into a remote canyon and left me with a pretty comfortable camp. After five days of scouring the canyon, I concluded the elk were somewhere else and so, the next day, I decided to pack out. I'd planned on making two trips out, over the rough trail, knowing each trip would take about three hours, one way.

With half the camp packed on my backpack, there was still a lot of room, so I just kept stuffing the bag and tying things on. I managed to get the entire camp on, but the pack ended up being huge! I guessed it weighed around seventy pounds, but when I weighed it later, it turned out to be ninety-eight pounds.

The very first part of the trip was the hardest. I had to climb up through an open avalanche chute to reach the faint trail leading out. Even though I could only climb fifteen to twenty yards at a time before having to rest, I still thought it would be quicker than making two trips. Besides that, the stubborn Edinger pride welled up once again. I wasn't going to let this pack beat me.

I had made it out over the toughest stretch of trail by mid-afternoon and had just gained an old, overgrown logging road, when I met another hunter, going in. I'd felt a little guilty about ruining this guy's plans and the first thing I did, even before dropping my pack, was apologize for doing so. No one would go into a spot like this just to kill an elk. No, when you hunt elk the hard way, you are after the total experience. I knew my being in there had ruined it for him. On the plus side, he wouldn't have to waste his time looking for elk where they weren't.

As we introduced ourselves, I was looking in his eyes, trying to read him the same way I used to do with dogs. His name slipped right past me. It wasn't long before we started swapping elk hunting stories and our passion for wild places. I told him about the first time I'd ventured into this canyon, which had turned into a real hunt from hell. Finally, I asked where he was from. When he replied, "Missoula," I said that the best hunting magazine I had ever read, *"Bugle"*, came out of there.

133

He replied, "Ya, I'm the conservation editor." So I asked him his name again, paying close attention this time. "Dave Stalling." Well of course I knew who he was then. I had been enjoying his articles!

Before Dave turned around and headed back out, with a pack one-third the size of mine, he told me I should write that story up and submit it. When I finally reached my truck, out by the gate, Dave had left a note on my windshield, urging me to stop at the Rocky Mountain Elk Foundation, before I left for home.

I did stop. Dave took me around and introduced me to the rest of the staff. There was big Don Burgess, the hunting editor, a man who looked like he could pack two elk quarters out at the same time; pretty and fit Jan Brocci, the managing editor; and the editor, Dan Crockett, a man about my size who looked like he ate nails for breakfast and his crushing handshake sealed that impression. Before I left, Dave urged me again to write that story. I told him I'd think about it.

Some months later, Dave used our meeting on the trail in one of his stories in *"Bugle"*. Here's how he described our encounter...

"From his looks and the amount of gear he carried, I figured he had been in the backcountry for weeks. The pack on his back was the size of a military foot locker, bulging at all sides as if it could burst open at any moment, with a canvas tent the size of a duffle bag tied to the top. I'd be reluctant to burden a mule with the load he carried."

Obviously I had left an impression on him. I guess I would write that story.

That's how my first published article in an outdoor magazine was born. Had I not met Dave, it would never have happened. Since then, Dave has moved on, but Don Burgess turned out to be such a nice fellow, that we became friends and I still stop to see the staff at the Elk Foundation every chance I get.

Following is the story, pretty much as it appeared in *Bugle* Magazine, of my first elk hunt in the Bitterroot Mountains. Like everything else in this book, it happened just as I lay it out, no exaggerating:

A Hunt From Hell

"We gotta get the hell offa here or we're all gonna die." Tom was scared. You could see it in his eyes. You have to be close to see fear in a man's eyes, and we were damn close. Even so, the blizzard raging around us on top of that exposed ridge was ripping away the words we were hollering.

"We can't get down here, it's too rocky," shouted Tom, "We'll have to follow along this ridge top to a place I know." With that he started out, leaning into the wind, trying to shield his face from the biting snow with me following and my wife, Leanne, falling in behind.

It's funny how life works. Because of a storm back home in Wisconsin four years earlier, here I was standing in the middle of another storm on top of this ridge in Montana. My house sat in the middle of a "downburst" – a straight-line wind that can travel for 100 miles, in a path four to five miles wide, with speeds of 90-plus miles per hour. That wind had flattened timber all around us, and since my main job is logging, it was an opportunity I took full advantage of. For three years I worked harder than I'd ever worked, and we were able to get some money ahead.

That's when my nephew, Tom Henderson, called from Montana. After high school he'd headed west to guide school, and now he was starting his own outfitting business. What better way to spend some of that money we'd saved? I decided to put in for a tag. If I drew, we'd join him after his last hunt and help pack out his wilderness camp, fitting in some elk hunting. We arrived in time to shake hands with his last hunter as he was leaving. Tom's plan was for us to leave long before dawn, hunt up a long elk-rich canyon that he hadn't yet ventured into, cross over the ridgewall and drop down to his camp by nightfall.

We were up at 3:00 a.m. and, after a 45-minute drive, we arrived at the gate. At that time, gates were a novelty to me. Although this Montana road went on another seven miles toward the wilderness boundary, some brave soul in the Forest Service had the backbone to put a gate here. Me and gates get along good. Every time I walk past one, I feel a sense of gratitude.

Tom and I slipped into our 40-pound packs, and Leanne strapped on a fanny pack carrying our lunches. Even though it was a day-hike into camp – which was stocked with plenty of food – we had to pack enough clothes, sleeping bags and gear for a six-day stay at camp. It was a real crispy morning, and it felt good to get underway.

By daylight, we'd climbed to where there was a little snow on the ground. We followed an old overgrown logging road that sidehilled into the canyon where Tom had seen all the elk sign. The road ended at a rock ledge, which gave us a beautiful view of the canyon. We could see all the way to the head, and Tom pointed out where we would have to go over the top. Leanne commented that it looked pretty steep. "A piece of cake," I replied. No point in making it any worse than it looked, I thought.

From there, the faint trail we followed ran basically level, intersecting the creek farther up the canyon. Since we had all day, we took a leisurely pace, stopping often to gossip about family and friends back home. After a while, we broke out onto an avalanche chute. I was amazed at the raw power represented by the tangled mass of broken trees at the bottom, and the delicate, clean-edged precision with which the avalanche had carved this path down the mountain. There was elk sign everywhere in the chute. Quietly, cautiously, we eased down it and crossed the creek.

It was close to noon and we had a view, so we decided to have lunch. Tom suggested we stay right there, build a lean-to and sleep on the ground. He was sure we could kill an elk that night. I figured he was right. But Leanne had her heart set on sleeping on a cot in a warm tent, so we reluctantly gave in.

While we ate, clouds were gathering up above, but no one paid any attention or cared. There were elk around and we were hunting now. After we ate, we slipped along on game trails, losing one for a while and then picking up another.

Within an hour it started to snow. Whenever we broke out of the timber, the falling snow obliterated any view of the head of the canyon. By 2:00 p.m. I began to wonder if we were going to make it to camp. The snow was falling very heavy at times now, and we had no idea how far it was to the head end.

It was closing in on 3:00 p.m. and we knew we weren't going to make it out of this canyon and over to camp by nightfall. As we broke out into an open area, Tom suddenly said, "There's an elk!"

The snow had let up a little, and I looked back to see him pointing up the hill. "Where?" I asked.

"Right there, don't you see them? There's a cow and a calf, and there's a bull right behind them."

I frantically scanned the hillside, finally spotting a cow and calf about 250 yards up the hill. "I see them," I said. "Where's the bull?"

"He just stepped into that strip of timber behind them. Get up there by that tree and get a good leaning rest!"

I quickly sneaked forward and lay down, getting a good rest for my '06. The cow spotted us and trotted off, angling uphill with the calf following. My eyes were trying to burrow holes through that little strip

136

of timber behind them when Tom shot. Boom. He shot again. "What the hell is he shooting at?" I thought. Boom, he shot a third time. There were a few moments of silence, and then Tom asked, "Why didn't you shoot?" "I didn't see anything," I replied.

It turned out the cow and calf I had spotted were not the same ones Tom had been pointing out. The bull he was shooting at was much farther up the hill. Leanne stayed at the bottom, as we took off uphill, to see if he had hit the bull.

By the time we reached the place where we thought the bull had been, it was difficult to tell for sure because our landmarks looked different up close. There were elk tracks all over and Tom started following a set he felt could be the right ones. I had a hunch the bull had been higher and kept climbing. After following a few false leads, I finally hit a track that told me I was on the right one. They turned uphill and then back towards a little strip of timber, which Leanne and Tom had last seen the bull go into. I began to think I was on the wrong tracks or Tom had missed because there was no blood or hair, cut by a bullet. Suddenly the trail turned sharply downhill. About 30 yards below was a big old log lying crosswise on the hillside, and as I got closer, I saw the snow brushed off the top and a wad of hair snagged by a knot. A healthy elk should have cleared this log easily. I put my thumb on the safety and got ready, easing up to the log, fully expecting to find the bull laying on the other side. There was nothing there, not even tracks. I backtracked a little. No, he hadn't doubled back. It was like he had turned into a bird and flown away.

A real thick patch of head-high spruce lay 15 feet below the log. I walked all the way around that patch. No tracks in, no tracks out. I got up on the log so I could look into the thicket, and suddenly I could make out the top tines of an elk antler. The bull had been running downhill, and with his last lunge, had caught his chest on that log, which had catapulted him into the thicket.

We cut some trees to free him. Tom looked down to the little orange speck at the bottom and said, "Poor Aunt Leanne, she must be freezing. We gotta hurry up and get down there and build a fire."

"How do we get the elk down there?" I asked.

"Aw, you just shove 'em down the hill. If you leave the guts in they slide easier."

So that's what we did. When he'd hang up, we'd go down to him, wiggle him loose and let him go again. Every once in a while the horns would clatter off the rocks and we would wince, but they made it. We dressed him out and found that one of Tom's bullets had hit the bull's heart, barely two inches from the bottom. Thankfully we had food for supper and breakfast; we were camping right there.

Tom was right about Leanne being cold. The storm had picked up again, so we found a flat spot between two trees where we could build a lean-to for shelter. Tom cleared the snow off the ground while Leanne and I gathered boughs and poles. In less than an hour we had a nice shelter with a fire going and enough wood for the night.

Tom went back to the elk with a flashlight and cut out the tenderloins, and we roasted them on a stick, caveman style. A little tinfoil, salt, and butter would have made it better, but as hungry as we were, we all agreed it was pretty darn good. Plus we didn't have to do dishes!

Between sweating and the snowstorm we were all pretty wet, so we hung up our outer clothes on the edge of our lean-to next to the fire and crawled into our sleeping bags with our long underwear on. Our body heat would dry the clothes next to our skin. Leanne and I zipped our

Tom's 'Hunt From Hell' bull.

bags together for added warmth. Tom had a good bag and wasn't worried. In two minutes the sucker was snoring! I swear, he could sleep on a rock!

The wind and snow kept me awake. It was about 3:00 a.m. when I finally drifted off into a sound sleep. I woke up just before daylight to find it had finally quit snowing and got the fire going again. Our clothes were a little drier, and after another meal of elk-on-a-stick, we got the bull quartered and hung up out of the reach of scavengers and tore down camp to leave no trace.

The weather was pretty nice-cloudy but not too cold. We could see the head of the canyon and felt we could be on top by noon. Tom thought I should lead in case we ran into another bull. So I started out in a foot of new snow. We were all feeling pretty good and we made good time, although the snow steadily got deeper.

By 11:00 a.m. it was snowing again. As we navigated across the bowl at the head of the canyon, the snow deepened, and the elk meat eaten that morning felt like it was just lying in the bottom of my stomach, giving me little energy. By the time we got to where the final uphill climb started, the snow was over our knees. I'd long since quit hunting, knowing it would be crazy to kill an elk up here.

According to the map we looked at later, we were facing a 1,450-foot climb on a hillside tilting at least 45 degrees. I started up and didn't get 30 yards before my legs got tired, really tired. I let Tom by to break trail. We reached a little bench and took a quick break. We were leaving the trickle of the creek, so we all took a good drink. Then Leanne made a wonderful announcement: she had squirreled away four bite-sized candy bars. I ate my portion as slowly as I could, trying to make it last. Man, it tasted good!

I took the lead again, but tired out quickly. I let Tom pass, wondering what was wrong with me. After another little break I tried to lead again. But this time, when I had gone even a shorter distance, I knew I was getting into trouble. When Tom went by, I told him he'd have to break trail the rest of the way – I just couldn't do it anymore. With a confident "Okay," he led out, with me stepping exactly in his steps and Leanne stepping into mine.

About a third of the way up, the storm intensified. We could barely see 40 yards and the wind was gusting worse. I got out my parka and put it on. Leanne added a nylon vest and Tom put on a heavier wool shirt. We asked Tom what he had for food at camp, and after he ran through the list, we all agreed peaches were the first thing we'd eat when we got there. Fantasizing about peaches, we started out again. With every step we were now sinking over our knees, not even touching bottom.

Suddenly I heard a roar approaching from the left. I knew it was wind, but I wasn't ready for what came with it. When it hit it nearly knocked us off our feet. The snow pellets hurled against our faces stung like a swarm of wasps. I threw up my shoulder and turned my face downwind. It only lasted for a few seconds and then was gone.

Our progress slowed to a snail's pace. It reminded me of those mountain climbers on television – one step, three panting breaths, another step, three more panting breaths. We began setting goals; "When we get to that rock, we'll rest. See that tree? We'll rest when we get there." The terrible gusts of wind kept roaring by, mostly from the left, but sometimes from the right. When we heard them coming, we crouched down as low as we could and protected our faces from those biting crystals.

Finally, we crawled to the crest. Most of the snow had blown off the ridge top, leaving only a foot to struggle through. It was flatter here and there was timber – all dead, ghostly, twisted white bark pine with an inch of ice frozen onto the windward side. Not a very cheerful place, but the going was easier. Soon it would be downhill!

When we hit the crest, the wind quit gusting from the left and right and screamed straight at us out of the northwest. (That's when Tom hollered, "We gotta get offa here or we're all gonna die.") I don't know what the miles per hour were, and I don't care to guess for fear you wouldn't believe me. We had to bend low and lean forward to stay on our feet. The ridge was really rocky there and soon narrowed, with a sheer drop off on both sides.

Leaning into the howling blizzard, we crept forward about 100 yards and came to a jagged little spot that we had to scramble down, clinging to the rocks. I heard Leanne holler, "I can't see!" I spun around to see her headed for a 10-foot drop.

"Stand still," I bellowed as loud as I could. When I got to her, the insides of her glasses were plastered full of snow. "Come on," I said, as I tucked her under my arm. "We gotta keep going or we're gonna lose Tom." He hadn't heard us and had kept going.

We couldn't have been 45 seconds behind him, but his tracks were already mere dimples in the snow. I was determined not to lose those tracks. "Come on Leanne, walk faster." We could pass within 20 feet of Tom in that whiteout and not see him.

Finally a dark form rose up from behind a rock; Tom had stopped and was using it for a windbreak. "We can get down here," he yelled. We joined him behind the rock, and Leanne cleaned the snow off her glasses. Then we picked our way down through a boulder field and soon came to where the ground, though still steep, was smooth, with hardly any trees or rocks. Tom figured we could sit on our butts and slide for a long ways, so we gave it a try. In no time we had gone over 300 yards and were down out of the fury.

We still had deep snow to contend with, and ahead was a tangled mass of an alder thicket. Anyone who's been in the mountains knows how miserable they are. While wiggling through that stuff, my legs finally gave out. I just couldn't go. While we sat there, Tom pointed out where camp was. I told him and Leanne to keep going. I had two sleeping bags, and if I wasn't down there by morning, to bring me some food when he came back up.

Sitting there by myself, I remembered all the times I'd been tired before. When I was ten, I started trapping beaver with my older brother. The snowshoes were nearly as tall as I was and he had worn me out many times, but never this bad. For the first time in my life, I had found my physical limit. Much like a marathon racer who "hits the wall", I got up, went a ways and rested, went a ways and rested. In about 45 minutes, I caught up to Leanne. Her legs were giving out, too.

After a while, we reached a strip of timber that led all the way to the canyon floor. There was hardly any snow under the trees and that helped immensely. The final push to camp came with darkness fast approaching. When we got to camp, Tom was coming up from the creek with a bucket of water. The snow had turned to rain down here, and he was shivering like crazy.

While he was down at the creek, the fire he'd started had gone out. As we took turns blowing on the coals to get it going again, Tom told how a fellow guide had thrown some white gas into an already warm stove to get it relit. Tom was just approaching the tent with his hunter when the match was lit. The stovepipe lifted off the launch pad 20 feet into the air and the tent walls blew outward. Throwing aside the tent flap, Tom found the stunned and singed, but otherwise unhurt guide, lying in one corner and the stove lying in the other.

We had a good laugh over that. Along with the laughter came relief that we had made it. Someone mentioned peaches, but to our surprise, no one was hungry! Too worn out to be. Later we had some Ramen noodles and went to bed.

The only answer I have to why we didn't turn back after Tom shot his bull is that it just wasn't our goal. That would have been like quitting! Almost as an afterthought, I shot a nice bull two days later. But the wilderness wasn't through with us yet. While packing out Tom's elk, we lost a mule when it slipped over the edge. It's a damn good thing elk hunting isn't always this hard.

My story was published in a special edition of "Big Weather" stories. Stalling later told me that the six that were published were selected from a large number of submissions. Since then, *"Bugle"* has published two more articles of mine. Publishing my stories, along with their encouraging words, helped give me the confidence that I could actually pull off writing this book.

Tommy's hunting country was a portion of the most rugged section of the Bitterroot Mountains. Lewis and Clark had taken the easiest route through these mountains and it had nearly killed them. Its sheer ruggedness had kept "progress" at bay long enough for a big chunk to be preserved by the Wilderness Act. I've gone back every year since that first hunt. The Selway-Bitterroot has sunk her teeth in me and she won't let go. Her pull is hard to explain. There were other years, like the first, where those mountains just kicked my butt, and I swore I wasn't going back, but by the time I was crossing North Dakota, on the way home, I was already planning the trip for next year. Its rugged beauty is part of it; the uncrowded conditions are another. Although it's a country made for young, hardy people, I was well into my forties when I took it on, and I swear, it has helped keep me young. I've found overcoming the challenges are hugely rewarding and the desire to run that country has given me enough incentive to stay in shape.

Perhaps Grandpa Walton (of the TV show *The Waltons*) said it best. "Life is like a mountain. When you come to one, you have two choices. You can either go over it or go around it. If you always take the easy way, you're going to miss the view from the top!" I have seen the view from the tops of mountains many times. The inspiring feelings are extraordinarily conflicting. The vastness around me make me feel so small and insignificant and yet, at the very same time, so important, for I may well be the only one of my species for miles around. It feels like everything I can see, I own, and I guess I actually do. We all do. There are so few places like this left. I believe we just have to keep them for future generations. I have never felt inspired in a shopping mall. I have only felt like one of the sheep.

A few years after my hunt from hell, I found myself in another tight spot in those mountains. I was elk hunting in early November and had spent most of the morning getting up into a little basin hanging high onto the side of this big canyon I was camped in. It looked like the perfect place for a big old bull to hole up in, before the heavy snows forced him down. Unfortunately for me, there were more of those places than there were big old bulls. Although it was a beautiful little place, all was quiet.

I'd found a game trail, sidehilling through that high basin, so I decided to follow it, as much exploring as I was hunting. There had been off and on snow squalls all day, so there was about two inches of soft snow on the trail. It would have been hard to make noise, even if I'd wanted to. As I approached this little bench, a place where the canyon wall came down, then flattened out, before dropping down to the creek far below, I cut some really fresh tracks that I took as a bobcat. We have them at home too, and the tracks were nice and round and about the same size as a really big male. There was quite a bit of small fir trees growing there and the tracks were everywhere.

As I reached the middle of that little bench, something went running off the edge, flying downhill. All I saw was a brief glimpse of its backline for about two jumps; a kind of rolling, bounding motion. I instinctively swung my gun around before wondering, "What the heck was that?" Just then I heard a sound, quartering off to my left. It reminded me of the sound of an airplane, when you first hear them, far in the distance.

As I swung my eyes to the left, to see what was making that noise, around a big Douglas fir, about twenty-five feet away, came a big momma mountain lion. She was growling, lips pulled back showing her teeth. Her ears were up and she was low to the ground, in either a stalking position or getting ready to pounce. In the whole time I'm telling this, the growling never stopped, it just got continuously louder.

My first reaction was, "Wow, a mountain lion!" I instantly knew what had happened. The thing I had glimpsed bounding down the hill and had made the tracks, was a young kit, about half grown. I had gotten too close before momma knew I was there, and now she wanted me out of there. She rolled a front paw forward and I thought if I threw something at her, I could scare her off. I quickly looked to my right, but there was nothing handy. When I looked back, she was taking another step forward and it suddenly occurred to me, "This is serious! You better get ready!"

In spots like this, my mind works really fast but everything else seems to happen in slow motion and I can remember every detail. It has to be the adrenaline. As I was bringing the gun up, I briefly thought about shooting next to her, to scare her. Even before the thought completely cycled through, I had dismissed it, knowing if it didn't work and instead triggered an attack, I would never be able to work the bolt fast enough before she would be on me. My next thought was, "I hope it's still not on nine power."

I had just been looking across the canyon at something and so I had cranked the scope up to nine power, the highest it would go. As my right eye settled behind the scope, it was on 9X all right, because all I could see was a blurry muzzle with barred white teeth! I followed the neckline down to where it started to broaden out, attaching to the shoulders. I held the crosshairs right there and thought, "It's your call." The next movement I saw was forward. Without thinking, I instinctively pulled the trigger.

Just like that, she was gone. I worked another shell into the chamber and waited for a little bit, ready to see what might happen, my whole body tingling with excitement. Finally, I backed up and moved to my left, getting higher so I could see over the edge of the bench. As I did so, I realized that it had never occurred to me to try to back out of there before, but even if it had, I wouldn't have done it. With mean dogs or mountain lions, it's the wrong thing to do. It only encourages them.

A few more steps, and I could make her out; her limp form sprawled across the snow. It came to me then that the pure, primitive feelings I had just experienced were thousands of years old. The ancient instincts hadn't changed. Not really having enough time to get scared, I had done what I needed to do to stay alive.

I thought, "Boy ain't this great! I'll be looking behind every tree for the rest of this hunt." Within an hour, I had convinced myself that it was a super rare occurrence, and it would never happen again.

Actually, it's not quite as rare as I thought. A year later, a fellow guide told me about how his brother had been knocked down by a female mountain lion, as he was hiking along a pack trail. When he fell, his gunstock broke. He was forced to grab the business end of his rifle and shoot from the hip, at point-blank range, as the big cat came back for him. She had two little kits with her. In this case, it's possible she was looking for something to eat.

A hunter I guided once said he had a friend who had to shoot one in the air, as it sprang for him, with his bow and arrow. He was into some elk and was cow calling, when he could hear a slight noise in the bushes coming his way. He knelt down on the logging road and drew his bow, expecting an elk, but instead, out popped a mountain lion. It swung its head towards him, spotted him, and sprang. His arrow caught it square and the big cat ran off, before it died.

I still do believe it was a rare occurrence, but since then, I've always tried to have at least a pistol on me, just to hedge my bet, when I'm in that country.

I found I enjoyed guiding for Tom. His hunting camp was a five-hour ride from the trailhead; far enough back to get the full flavor of wilderness. The hunters were as diverse as you can imagine; highly educated to almost uneducated, filthy rich to a common man, short and

144

fat to tall and skinny. But with all their differences, you could count on someone in every camp making the same comments.

Someone would always observe how clean it was along the pack trail. I guess they expected the trash they were used to seeing along our roads and hiking trails in our parks. I've found it's the wilderness traveler who is most likely to push the candy bar wrapper back into their pocket. That's just the kind of people wilderness attracts. I had a few hunters I had to tell to pick up their wrapper, but not many.

Someone would always comment about how many stars there were in the sky. I guess the pollution or city lights blocked them out where they lived. And someone would always comment about, if it weren't for an occasional jet flying over, you wouldn't even know there was an outside world. That told me that they were getting the experience that I hoped they would, out of their hunt.

The one I always enjoyed the most and I was actually laying for, was the inevitable question, "What happens if you have a heart attack way back here?" I had to fight to keep a straight face, as I led them outside the tent. There was always a big log, laying around someplace close by, and I

Me in the Selway-Bitterroot Wilderness.

would point to it and say, "As soon as you're dead, we lay you over that log, so when you stiffen up, we can pack your body out on a mule." Most of the guys then saw the humor in their question. A few got a sour look on their face and so I tried to reassure them by saying we wouldn't really lay them over that log. We were skilled enough to "mantie" (wrap in canvas) a warm body on a mule and they could stiffen up on the way out!

Did they really expect a rescue chopper would land in the meadow in five minutes? This was before satellite phones were invented, but even now, if you had one of those phones in camp, it would still probably take an hour before emergency medical help arrived.

Every wilderness visitor needs to understand that the known and unknown dangers of wilderness travel are simply the price of admission.

If you can't accept calculated risk, then you had better stay on your couch, in front of the TV.

I also enjoyed watching their personalities change, especially the ones who thought they were important. It usually took only a day, maybe two; when you could see those airs just melt away. They just relaxed into their real selves. I think they began to connect with the real world we were in; where discrimination does not exist, because nature treats everyone equally. I don't care if you're standing next to the most famous or richest person in the world, the sun shines on you equally, and the rain falls on you equally. Some of the deeper thinkers even realized the commonality we have with all living things; that we are all on this planet just trying to stay alive as long as we can.

One of my hard-earned bulls of the Selway-Bitterroot.

They also came to understand that neither they, nor their fearless guides, were in control. The weather, the elk, even the docile animal they rode in on, had a mind of their own. That lack of control was too unsettling for a few, and Tom would take them out early, either to go home or have a more controlled hunt, down in the valley. I found that if you really want to get to know a person, live with them in the backcountry for a week. You'll find the real person, unfiltered.

I spent a lot of time with almost all my hunters sitting and glassing, trying to spot an elk or waiting for one to come out of the timber. The conversations, after a few days of getting to know each other, became heartfelt and personal. I'm sure we talked about things they had never talked to their wives or best friends about. Many of the wealthier clients said they envied me; that I could be doing this. I got the strongest impression from some of those guys, having had quiet time to reflect on the important things in their life, that they felt trapped in their daily lives. It also made me feel like I was doing something right; that there was more to life than money.

One of the last hunters I guided was a recently retired cop from the Detroit, Michigan, area. Somehow, some wires got crossed and he showed up a week too early, so Tom had me take him into a secluded canyon with backpacks. Compared to our regular hunting camp, this one was pretty rustic. We camped near two avalanche chutes, where avalanches come down on a regular basis every winter, keeping a grassy area open where elk like to feed. After a day when nothing came out on those slides, I tried to take him farther up the canyon, where we'd seen and killed elk before, but he had a hard time getting around in that rough country. We ended up watching those two slides the rest of the hunt. We'd get up at daylight and watch until about 9:00, then we'd have breakfast. The middle of the day was spent reading, telling stories and napping, before going back for the evening watch. As we were packing out, he told me it was the best hunt he had ever been on, even though we had never even seen an elk. Except for the elk thing, I had enjoyed it too. He had been good company.

On the trip out, there was a knob sticking out into the canyon, with a view both ways; up the canyon, where we had been, and down to the civilized valley. I had just finished pointing out some places of interest up canyon and when I turned around, to look down into the valley, the sun glinted off the windshield of a car, way down there on the highway. It hit me like someone had punched me in the stomach. I could just imagine those people hurrying around down there like a bunch of ants and I did not want to go back to that world and become another one of those scurrying ants. I had to fight the urge to run right back up the canyon. I did not want to go back to that world. In only a week, I had gotten "bushy", just like I used to on the Yukon. I think I could become a hermit real easy.

So far, I've never been able to talk Leanne into another elk hunt with me, after our hunt from hell. What we did manage to do, with her blessings, was to buy our own stock, a five-horse trailer and a truck to pull it, and all the gear we needed to go out to the Bitterroots on summer camping trips every year. We started going on those summer trips in 1995, when our boy, Garret, was eight. Leanne missed a few years after our daughter was born, but since the age of three, Aubrey too, has been going along. The first few years, she rode in the saddle in front of me, then we got a buddy saddle and she rode behind Leanne. Now Aubrey rides her own mule.

These summer pack trips into the mountains are very relaxing and enjoyable. We pack into different places where there is grazing for the stock, different lakes to fish in, and various trails to ride. Some days we just go for a trail ride, some days we just fish, catching enough for supper, some days we just lay around camp and read and take naps. We seek out the harder to reach places, far enough from the trailhead where others usually don't go. Sometimes we have a little company, but I have yet to run into a jerk in the backcountry. Everyone is polite, helpful when they can be, and respectful of one another's space. We are all there for the same reason, to seek solitude.

Our pack string switch-backing up a mountain in the Selway-Bitterroot Wilderness.

The hard part on these trips is getting in. The budget of the Forest Service to maintain the pack trails has been drastically cut. For people like us, who go into the less popular places, that means we usually have to cut out the trails ourselves, by hand, because motorized tools are prohibited.

In 2009, there was an unusually high amount of down timber across the trails from a very heavy, wet snowstorm, which hit late in the winter along the spine of the Bitterroot Mountains. Our trip in, that mid-July day, was made even more miserable from the cold, wet rain that was falling. Leanne had wanted to spend another day at the trailhead to wait for the weather to clear, but I overruled her. We only had three weeks, and I wanted to spend every day we could in the high-country. By the time we were half way in, on the eight-hour ride, we were pretty wet, despite our raincoats. Up high, it was raining harder and much colder. I would not have been surprised to see snowflakes. Leanne and Aubrey had to get off and walk often, so they could get warm. From clearing trail, I alternated from sweating to freezing.

Leanne is still not a whiner, so as we were setting up the wall tent, in the place we were going to stay for a week, I asked her, "As you looked ahead, watching me lead the pack string coming in, what were you thinking back there? Were you cussing me out for dragging us in here in the rain, or were you proudly thinking, 'Yes, that's my man'!" Not one to ever let my head get too big, she simply said, "I figured you'd get us in here, one way or another." I guess she had confidence in my stubborn determination she has seen too many times.

It had been hard for me. Leanne helped clear trail when she could, but by the time she got her gelding tied up and made her way up past the pack string, I would have the smaller stuff cleared, so I only motioned her up when we had to uncase the two-man crosscut saw. Constantly getting off and on my mare, throwing stuff out of the trail and trying to keep my balance on the steep hillsides had been really hard with just one good leg. Well, now I'm getting ahead of myself. I guess now would be a good time to go back to the very beginning of this book and finish that story; the reason so many people insisted I had a great story to tell.

Chapter 10

WILL TO LIVE

So that you don't have to flip back to Chapter 1, let me reacquaint you with my life as it was on February 15, 2007, the day of my terrible logging accident. My life was good. With all the hard work Leanne and I had done, we were out of debt and had some money put away for a rainy day. Our son Garret had finished tech school as a diesel mechanic and was working over in Green Bay and Aubrey was in the third grade, getting great reviews from her teachers. You would think, by now, that I would have started to back off from that determined Edinger tenacity, to see how far I could get, but a person's genetic makeup doesn't change. I was taking more time to play, but even then I was still playing hard.

Although it was physically demanding, I really enjoyed my work as an independent logger. I had cultivated a good working relationship with landowners, wood buyers, foresters and my trucker by keeping my word and logging in a manner that was best for the land and the environment. Logging is still a destructive endeavor but I readily adopted the practices that would have the least impact on the ecosystem. Between not looking for an excuse to skip work and that hardheaded determination to overcome the challenge of the bitter cold, I never gave serious thought to staying home that day.

From the previous forecasts, I knew that an arctic blast of cold air would sweep across northern Wisconsin. When Leanne told me that morning that it was 40 below, I was not surprised. I had been preparing myself mentally to meet the challenge of the cold, the same as I had done many times before. Knowing from experience how to dress for those temps, I had an extra pair of quilted long johns already laid out and packs of chemical hand warmers already bought.

The logging job I was working on was way east of Phillips. The land belonged to my brother-in-law, Bill Heindl, my sister Betty's second husband. I had already done a lot of work for Bill. He said he liked the work I did and that he could trust me to treat the land right, a trust I worked extra hard not to betray.

I was really excited about the coming Saturday night. I belonged to

150

a county-wide lake and river protection association and we were going to have a social gathering where I was going to call square dances. On the hour-and-a-half drive to work that morning, I had a pair of CD headphones on, listening to fiddle music while I practiced my calls. To reach my job site, I turned off County D and Chequamegon Drive onto Forest Service Road 130. I generally navigate by landmarks, not road signs but just two weeks before it had dawned on me that I didn't know the Forest Road's # and thought that, in case of emergency, that number might come in handy. I memorized it easily as the same as the time 1:30 in the afternoon.

Five minutes after turning onto Forest Road 130, I pulled up alongside my diesel-powered skidder. It started easily, after I circulated the warm engine coolant from my pickup through the skidder motor for about ten minutes with a pair of quick-couple hoses.

I use a pole skidder, sometimes called a cable skidder, for logging. Compared with current technology, it's the hard way to log, but it has some advantages, one being it keeps me in shape. Here's how it works: After cutting a bunch of trees down with a chainsaw, trying to fall

Me with my pole skidder before the accident.

them in a direction so they can be pulled out easily, I back the skidder into position so that, as I pull out a long cable (mainline) attached to the winch mounted on the back, I can hook onto several trees at a time. Sliding on the mainline are chokers, short cables that I hook around the butt of each log. Back on the skidder, I winch the logs ahead until they reach the back of the skidder. Then I cut the limbs off with the chainsaw. With the tops being all together, it saves time and energy. Then I drag them out to the landing, unhook the logs and roll them into a pile with the blade. Once in the pile, I cut them into eight-foot lengths so that my trucker can easily load and haul them to a mill.

So, that morning, I had just finished limbing my second skid and was falling trees for the next one. My body had not warmed up from the work yet. (I guessed the temps to still be about 15 below.) The first tree I cut was actually four stems growing out of one stump. Soft maples commonly grow that way. In the winter, because those stems are frozen together, you can fall them as if they are one tree. If you try that in the summer, they'll peel apart like a banana and you'll be dead real quick. So, that clump fell where I wanted it to, then I went over to the next.

That one was a double. The one in front, the way I wanted it to fall, was much smaller than the twenty-inch in diameter one that grew behind. The two stems separated at eyeball level. I glanced at the top and knew instantly it already wanted to fall, naturally, the way I wanted it to go. I made just a tiny mistake here. I misjudged how top heavy it was, how badly it wanted to fall that way, which put way more tension on the wood fiber down at the base than I realized. Had it occurred to me that they might split apart, I would have cut them differently.

I notched the small one, in front, almost all the way through to the seam. As I swung the saw around to the backside and began sawing through the bigger one, I still had square dance calls going through my head. "Wave to your partner as you go by, catch the next on the fly. Gents turn out and ladies in, all join hands and go ag...." All of a sudden the butt of the big tree quickly started to "barber-chair," splitting vertically up the trunk, throwing the bigger portion of the butt high into the air. When that happens, it's always bad, because you don't know where the tree is going to go.

My saw came free from the cut immediately. (Loggers are notorious for stupidly hanging onto a pinched saw, staying dangerously close to the falling trunk, hoping the saw will come loose before the tree hits the ground, likely smashing it.) I pivoted around to my right and took off running, but already the butt of the tree was shoulder high and traveling backward. The only escape route I had was a narrow gap between the end of the tree I had cut just before and its stump. My right leg sprang through the gap and my trailing left leg was just beginning to clear the stump when, BOOM #*#*!!

There was no pain, just a stunning jolt that ran through my whole body. I remember dropping the saw as I was jerked backwards, my arms flailing around, trying to keep my balance. I ended up sitting astraddle the butt of the tree I had been running past, although I never realized it until later, when I saw the pictures. Initially I thought I had sat down on a cradle knoll (a small mound of earth). That's how stunned I was!

My first instinct was to touch my chest with my right hand. Subconsciously, I believe I thought I was dead. I almost expected not to

1   2

The accident scene in the Wisconsin woods where I almost lost my life. Note the bloodstain on the stump at lower center. Points of interest include:

1 – Clump I ended up sitting astraddle of.

2 – Stump my left leg was trying to clear when the tree hit.

3 – The tree that kicked sideways and sheared my left leg off.

4 – Where the accident started.

5 – Small, hung-up leaner that kicked the tree sideways.

Also, please see full color photograph of this scene on Page 97

feel it, but my chest was solid and I thought, "Oh, you're all right." My right leg was out in front of me, and as I pulled it back slightly, I went to push up with my left, to stand, but nothing happened. I tried again, putting real effort into it this time, feeling my thigh move, but again nothing. As I was bringing my eyes around to see what was wrong, I was mentally preparing myself to see a broken leg. What I saw instead just hammered me. Just below my knee, I had no leg! It was gone! Sheared right off! For a fraction of a second, before my brain went into denial, I realized I would never be perfect anymore, that thousands of years of evolution and fifty some years of moving across the landscape with grace and balance was gone. Steam was rising off the end of the stump and I could see a stream of blood, about the size of a pencil, arcing down into the snow. Then I spotted my boot, lying there on the snow, twisted backwards, with something white sticking out the top! I jerked my eyes away; my head was swimming; I couldn't focus. All I wanted to do was to wake up from this awful nightmare.

I'm not sure how much time passed, a few seconds – maybe thirty. My first rational thought was, "You gotta get going here." That was the moment that I accepted it. It was done. Now what? My plan for a bad chainsaw cut was to use my belt as a tourniquet. As I grabbed my thigh and swung it over the log, to slide down onto the ground, wild fear was boiling inside of me. All I wanted to do was holler, but having a plan and having to focus on it somehow kept it at bay. The pain was just starting to come now. *I made a snap judgment that a half-hour was all I had before I bled to death.* I suppose that call came from years of tracking mortally wounded game. How long I would stay conscious was anyone's guess. Another flash, almost an aerial view, of how far away the nearest help was, made me positive that getting out of there alive was impossible if I didn't get the bleeding stopped. Adrenaline was pouring through my veins now and I was thinking really fast. I was not sorting through options, like a reasoning person would. Whatever came into my mind, I went with it.

I slid off the tree onto the snow, my boot dragging along because it was still attached by shreds of clothing. I whipped my gloves off and jerked my belt free. I put it around my leg, just above the knee, strung it through the buckle, and gave it a good reef. Between the age of my belt and the strength the urgency gave me, the belt broke. "Shit".... The only thing to do was to tie the damn thing back together and try it again. I had to stop my life from leaking out the bottom of my leg! I was right on the edge of panic and the knot came apart when I tried to jerk it tight. "Focus." I tried it again, making sure I tied a square knot, holding onto the ends as I pulled it tight. My fingers felt like stubs, from the cold, and I briefly thought of Jack London's story, "To Build a Fire". It felt like this was my last chance to get it right.

Once again around my leg, I gave it another reef. I couldn't go easy. I had lots of clothes and muscle to squeeze off. This time I jerked the buckle right off the belt! I realized then I was going to die. For a few precious seconds, I quit. The words of resignation formed in my mind; "The heck with it. Just lay back and get cold."

As I settled back on my elbows and stared blankly at the sky, I felt the panic and the fight leaving my body. In its place came the deepest sense of despair you could ever imagine. I had never felt so alone. It seemed like my fighting spirit was replaced by darkness. Perhaps I began to pass out. I'm not sure about that; I just remember that I saw a blackness. Suddenly, out of nowhere, unspoken words came to me. "What the heck! Why don't you see how far you can get?"

Boy, hadn't I spent my whole life seeing how far I could get. Always wanting the deer stand the farthest back in the woods, struggling for years to see how far I could get in the sled dog racing game, trying to see how long I could stay awake on marathon trips, to find the limit of how much I could pack on my back. I had never shrunk from a physical challenge before. Why should now be any different? I think, in reality, I just really wanted to live. My fight, and unfortunately the panic, came roaring back. I still knew I was going to die. I was just going to go until I couldn't anymore, just like a good sled dog. Laying back and getting cold would have been too boring and easy. I have to do everything the hard way.

As I went to roll onto my knees, I prepared myself for the extra pain that would come with moving, a flashing memory of Brian Edinger, when he had that broken leg a few years earlier. I was relieved to find that there was no extra pain when I moved. I stuffed my hands back into my gloves, feeling the welcome warmth of the heat packs inside. It was then I noticed my chainsaw still idling right next to me. As I was leaning forward to shut it off, I remember thinking how stupid it was to care if it was shut off, before I left, but I couldn't stop myself.

So I started crawling to my idling skidder, 150 feet away. The pain was coming really strong now. As I was crawling, a vision of people saying that they found me crawled halfway to the skidder, or slumped over the steering wheel of the skidder, pushed up against a tree, and saying, "but he was trying; he never quit!" came to me. You can't imagine how that Edinger pride welled up inside of me, giving me strength; it just lifted me right up. While I was crawling I was not thinking about how I was going to get into the skidder, I just kept crawling, leaving a bloody smear in the snow with my boot dragging along behind, still attached by the many layers of shredded clothes.

My skidder is hard to get into. The first step is above one's knee plus the cab is tight. Using my hands, I wedged my way up between the tires. Then standing on my good leg and holding my severed foot against my chest with my left hand, so it wouldn't get tangled in the brush, I put my bad knee on the left side of the step. I raised myself up with my right arm until I could get my foot alongside my knee and started to stand. My foot slipped off the first time and I fell back down, stubbing my bloody stump on the skidder. I cried out from the pain. Back to focusing; placing my knee farther to the left to give my foot more room for purchase; placing my boot with a cleat inside the steel bar. Once I was up, I laid my foot on the running board and wiggled and squiggled my way up into the seat. My skidder has a power shift transmission, which is an automatic with a

155

clutch, so I just threw it into gear, pressed on the accelerator, and headed out to my pickup 300 yards away.

On the way out, the trees weren't standing straight up and down a few times, but somehow I got it back. When it looked like I was going to make it to my truck, I gave a little thought to what I should say when I reached 911. I didn't want to sound like a lot of others on TV hysterically shouting, "Help-help-help!" It felt like I could pass out at any time, so I figured if all I said was I was on Bill Heindl's land, they would find me. Everyone knows Bill; he owns the funeral home in Phillips.

To my surprise, I reached the logging road. I had to stop short and leave enough room so I could get by my skidder with my pickup. I scrambled down out of the cab and crawled the fifty feet to my truck, leaving another bloody smear behind. Getting in the truck was easy but it has a standard transmission. As I laid my boot on the floor and pushed in the clutch with my right foot, my eye caught the four- wheel drive shift lever. Just like that I rammed it into 4WD Low, knowing the motor wouldn't kill when I let the clutch out in first gear. I think you could spin the tires, while idling, with that gear ratio! As I passed my skidder, I briefly glanced below the cab. The entire side was covered with frozen, caked on blood! After I shifted into second, I dug into my lunch box and grabbed my cell phone. In an area where the signal had always been non-existent, my 911 call got through. The gal working the emergency dispatch at the Sheriff's office that morning was Deputy Joanne Heitkemper. When I heard her voice, hope began to creep in. Maybe I was going to make it.

Here is the conversation, word for word, taken from the recording:

911-State your emergency------------------Hello---Hello
Hello, can you hear me?
I can – go ahead.
Hi, I'm Gary Edinger – I cut my leg off – I need help.
OK – where are you at.
I'm on Bill Heindl's land out in Emery----ah, off of 130-----hah, south of- 130--- off of-- Chequamegon Drive (The pain was so bad, I was having a hard time talking.)
So D to Chequamegon Drive?
Go to Chequamegon – Drive, south on – 130--three quarters of a mile.
Is your truck or anything on the roadway?
I'm – I'm trying to drive out – now.
You're driving right now?!!

Real slow — My leg is completely cut off.

Where's your leg at?

Huh – aah – huh (heavy breathing) – It, it's in my Goddamn boot!! (She didn't ask where my boot was.)

OK, and – are you bleeding real bad?

YES!!

OK, just one second.

I'm going to pass out!

Well stop driving, pull over to the side of the road. What kind of vehicle do you have?

It's a Toyota pickup.

What color?

Green.

OK, pull over to the side of the road.

I ain't pulling over; I'm getting out of here!

Where you gonna go?

I'll be on D if I can get there!

OK, just one second.

I don't have a f---ing second! (I was frustrated. Why was she asking all these questions? Just send help)

Then the Deputy, Brian Roush, got on the phone. He had just come into the office from the garage and could tell from the sound of Joanne's voice that something serious was going on. As Joanne went to scramble the ambulance and a rescue chopper from Marshfield, she handed the phone to Brian.

Hello, this is Brian.

Huh?

Who am I speaking with? Gary Edinger?

Gary Edinger, ya.

OK-------OK I'm going to stay on the line with you. Where are you at right now?

Driving out of the woods.

Driving out of the woods?

Ah huh.

Aw, what part of the county are you in? What road?

I'm going to be on 130-----off of Chequamegon drive.

OK

Oh God it hurts.

Is there anybody with you at all?

No.

OK. Ahm, when you go off Chequamegon Drive on 130, how far south are you?

Three-quarters of a mile.

OK. Are you still on the woods road?

Yes.

OK

I've got it in low (4X Low) so I'm driving slow.

OK. Now which direction does the woods road go off of 130, to the east or to the west?

It goes to the west. It's the only one.

OK

I don't know—If I—I get bad reception I might lose ya.

OK. No, we got a really good connection right now, so just stay on the line with me Gary.

Oh! Oh God it hurts! (More heavy breathing. The pain seemed to come in waves.)

You cut your leg with the saw?

No, a tree severed it right off. I mean it's right off. It's just sittin' in my Goddamn boot.

OK. How – is it below the knee?

Yes.

OK.

I couldn't get a tourniquet on it; my belt broke.

OK.

I'm going to bleed to death if they don't hurry.

OK. We've got them en route as quick as they can go. Joanne's got the ambulance paged.

They can't get here fast enough, man.

I know, Gary, I know what you're saying. We'll get out there as fast as we possibly can, OK?

Oh! What a stupid ass mistake. Oh God – If I don't make it, tell my wife and family I love them. Tell them I'm sorry – I'm so sorry.

OK, we'll do that, we'll do that. Umm, you said a tree had fell on it?

(A bunch of heavy breathing, I was losing signal)

Are you all right Gary? Are you with me?

(Some more heavy breathing)

Gary?

Yes.

Are you still with me?

I can't hear ya.

OK, are you still driving?

Yes.

OK.

Oh! Oh God it hurts. Oh, why me. What a dumb ass mistake.

OK, Joanne's got the ambulance en route; she's got 'em paged. Are you still driving towards the woods – are you still driving towards the town road?

I'm almost there. (The signal is breaking up now)

You're almost to the town road?

Yes.

OK. What color pickup do you have?

What?

What color pickup do you have?

It's a Toyota green pickup.

Green?

Green, dark green.

Dark gray, OK.

Then there was a lot of one-sided talking with Brian and somebody in the office. In the background you can barely hear a lot of grunting and moaning from me, my phone breaking up. Brian came back…

Are you still there Gary? Can you hear me?-------Gary?------Gary?

UH!

Can you still hear me?

A little bit.

A little bit, OK.

I'm on the town road.

You're on the town road?

I got it in third gear now.

Excuse me?

I got it in third gear now, going a little quicker.

You're on the town road, excuse me, on 130?

It's hard to shift w-t- jus- -n- (That was the last words they could make out)

Which direction you going, Gary? Gary, can you hear me?

Brian is talking to Joanne now, telling her I was on the town road but he had lost the cell phone signal. He was racing out to meet me. (There was seventeen miles of country roads between us.) Joanne came back on the phone.

OK, are you there Gary?

(Every once in a while she could hear me moan.)

Are you there Gary? Gary?

Oh! Ahh!

You're breaking up Gary, stay on the line though.

Oh!

OK Gary, I'm with you. Are you on 130, or are you on Chequamegon Road?

Uh!

Gary, you with me yet?

Gary you there yet?

Gary you there yet?

That was the last of trying to talk for a while. I knew I was going to lose them, and was gratefully surprised that I had been able to talk that long. The pain reached its highest point during this stretch. I knew as I slipped into deeper stages of shock, the pain would diminish. I also knew I could get signal again right when I broke over the hill, just before I got to county road D, a mile and a half away. I had driven out there many times before, to call out.

As I broke over the hill I tried three times to dial 911. Every time I put the phone to my ear, I just heard a "bleep". The last time, I looked at the screen and it said 916! "Focus." I took my mind off driving and concentrated on pushing those three little numbers, 9-1-1-send. The phone rang…

911

I'm on – Gary Edinger – I'm back.

Where are you at Gary?

I'm on D right now, which way should I go? (I didn't know if the Prentice or Phillips ambulance was responding. I thought perhaps I might have to go towards Brantwood. She didn't know what I was thinking and it momentarily threw her.)

Well----head towards Phillips.

OK. I got my directionals on.

Your 4-ways you mean?

Yes.

OK. So you're on county D, David, right now.

That's correct.

OK. Just stay on the line with me, stay on the line with me.

160

Should I stay on the road?

Stay on the road, but stay on the line with me.

Should I get help?

Well, we have an ambulance en route and we have a squad en route. Ahm, why don't you pull over to the side of the road?

I can't hear you, try it again.

Why don't you pull over to the side of the road. The ambulance is en route.

I'll s--- -- --bert Dunbar's', okay? (Breaking up)

You'll – where?

(More heavy breathing) Uh! Oh God it hurts.

Gary, why don't you pull over to the side of the road.

I'll – I'll – I'll stop – at –Robert Dunbar's, I'll see if he's home.

No, no, you just stay in the truck. Stay in the truck Gary.

Ya I will, but (she cut me off)

Don't even go in the driveway, we want to find you. Just stay right on county D and why don't you park alongside the road.

 (I thought to myself, geez lady, I told you whose yard I'd be in!)

(She talks briefly to the ambulance, telling them my current position on the radio.)

Gary, listen to me, don't pull in a driveway.

I'm still going towards Phillips.

OK, stay on county D. I don't want you in a driveway, 'cause they might miss you.

(I obeyed the order not to pull into Dunbars' yard while completely ignoring her directives to pull over because that fit into seeing how far I could get.)

How close are they?

They're on their way. They're leaving Phillips and I have a squad en route also.

Oh f--- it hurts.

I know it hurts. That's why I want you to pull over before you pass out and then hit somebody.

I ain't going that fast!

Well, I don't care. Why don't you pull over to the side of the road, stay right on D and pull over to the side of the road.

I'm still OK.

I know you're .... I know you're panicking, and I know it hurts, but we gotta find you.

161

You'll find me; I'm on the road.

OK, well stay on the road and pull over to the side.

Ohh! Ohh! If I—If I stop doing something it's going to be worse. Ohh! (I guess Joanne understood that or she finally gave up, because that was the last time she asked me to pull over. Why I never stated the obvious, that I knew I needed every minute I could get, baffles me.)

Stay with me though.

Um humm. (Then a little break in time.)

So, are you still driving?

Yes.

OK.

(Some more moaning)

Was there anybody else out in the woods with you?

No, too ornery to work with anybody else.

OK. (She made a little laugh)

Today it would have been OK though. Today I needed help, finally. Oh, I'm going to lose my leg.

Hang in there; hang in there with me.

Ohh, I need my leg.

I know, I know, you got it there. As long as you – we'll get to you, hang in there.

It's not even on.

They can do a lot of stuff now days. Don't you be worrying about that right now. We gotta get you help and stop that bleeding.

If I don't.....(Here's the only place I guess I went off into la-la land. I would swear I continued to say: – "make it, tell my wife how much I love her. I couldn't have asked for a better wife. Tell Garret how proud I am of the way he turned out. Tell Aubrey to grow up straight and tall, like her brother." **Joanne said, "You're going to make it."** I said, "Promise." **She replied, "I promise."** Except for the first three words, none of it is on the tape.)

Hang in there Gary. Do you know where you're at right now?

I'm almost to Morey's.

Almost to Morey's?

Almost to Morey's, 10-4.

So, you're coming to a corner there, be careful on the corner.

It's a ways.--------Ohh! Gosh, you know how hard it is to walk without a leg?

Well, let's get the bleeding stopped and get you to a hospital. They

162

can do wondrous things now.

I had to crawl up in my damn skidder.

You had a skidder out there?

(A bunch more moaning) Thanks for helping.

OK, just hang in there, hang in there. Did you round the corner by Martins Drive there yet?

No, I'm not to Morey's yet. Not going fast enough. (There were times in here where my arm was doing all the steering while my mind drifted, just like that time on the Alaska Highway. I never did stop to shift it into high range, so I never got going any faster than 25 MPH, but it sure seemed more like 45 to me.)

OK. Do you feel like you're going to pass out?

I'm getting pretty light. I suppose I'm going into shock.

I'm sure; you're probably losing a lot of blood. Did you wrap it with anything?

My damn belt broke, twice. I got enough sense to put a tourniquet on, but I don't have anything anymore.

So, do you have anything on it right now?

No. I can't find anything, there's nothing in the truck. (Right about in here I sneaked a peak on the floor, to see how much blood was there. There looked like about three cups, mostly already coagulated or frozen. That gave me hope. Had I known the truth, that I was running on empty, perhaps that would have been too much.)

Well, unless you stop, don't even try to put anything on it anymore.

Well of course, I ain't that dumb!

Well, you know, when you start going into shock, you don't think of everything.

Where are they?

They're on their way out there.

How far now? How close?

Well, the officer is probably just a mile or two from you.

Oh good. I need someone to lean on. Oh! Oh shit! Maybe you better call my wife. (I began to think my odds of making it were getting pretty good.)

OK, what . . .

Do you know where she works?

What's her number?

Leanne, she works at the Medford Clinic, er, the Prentice, Prentice Clinic. She'd probably want to know.

163

OK, just one second, just one second, OK?
(Some more moaning. A good friend, Butch Lobermeier, listened to the tape and commented here that it sounded like I was drunk. Well I was, sort of. Just like a drunk, my brain was starving for oxygen.)
Can you hear me yet?
OK, Gary?
Yes?
Can you hear me now?
I'm going around the corner now. I'm headed for DeLeasky's.
So, you're on Martin's Drive corner.
I'm not on Martin's Drive; I'm on D, headed for DeLeasky's. Here he comes, here he comes. I see him.
552, you're meeting with him now.
I see him, I see him.
10-4, 552, he sees you there.
All right, I'm shuttin' 'er off. Copy?
OK, what was that?
I'm done, bye.
OK, thank you, Gary. Good luck.
No, thank you.

The call consumed seventeen minutes. A good guess at the total elapsed time, from when the tree hit to when Brian got to me, would be right at twenty-seven minutes. I had driven five miles. In the time it took me to drive the last four, Brian had driven thirteen. His car looked like a ten foot high tornado coming at me 100 miles an hour, the road debris swirling up behind, with lights and sirens flashing at its base. What a relief it was to meet him! I figured now that I was going to live. (I really wasn't out of danger.) When I started out, I was going to be like a good sled dog, going until I couldn't go anymore. As it turned out, I would have been a great sled dog, I never tipped over.

With tires squealing, the squad car swung in behind me. I don't know what I was going to do, but I was in the process of getting out of my truck when he reached me. "No, no, stay in your truck," as he grabbed his belt and wrapped it around my leg. He pulled on it hard, three times, before he got the bleeding stopped. A passerby stopped and offered his help. Brian had him get his portable radio, from the front seat, so he could talk with the ambulance I guess. Brian told me later that I wasn't making much sense; I kept talking about dancing.

In about five minutes, the ambulance crew arrived. They threw a stretcher down on the blacktop and helped me lay down on it. I felt them lift my short leg and cut the clothing still attached to my boot. Then I heard someone say, "Hang onto him." Brian had his right hand locked in mine and he said, as he leaned over my chest, "Look at me Gary, look at me." All of a sudden, this terrible, excruciating pain hit the end of my leg. They just started wrapping gauze around the end of that raw stump. I hollered as loud as I could. That also woke me up pretty good! They threw me in the ambulance and away we went towards the Phillips Airport, where the flight for life chopper would pick me up.

I remember them asking if I was hurt anywhere else. Then they asked, like three different times, if I had been drinking in the last twenty-four hours. It was as if they couldn't believe a logger didn't drink! Someone had a pair of big scissors and made like he was going to cut off my good wool shirt. I sat up off that stretcher spouting, "No, no. Look, there's just a few buttons!" and tried to show them how to unfasten a button. "Okay, okay Gary, lay back down. We just need a little skin." They got my left shoulder bare enough to attach some monitoring pads.

After I convinced them my wool shirt was sacred, things calmed down. I had made it out of the woods, I had seen how far I could get, and now all I wanted to do was escape from reality and pass out. In a perfect world, I figured I would wake up in the hospital, with my leg sewed back on. I relaxed every pore in my body and tried to slip away. Those suckers started pestering me. "Come on Gary; keep your eyes open Gary." Then they started asking me questions like how old I was, my wife's name, did I have kids, what were their names. I was glad they didn't ask for anniversary or birth dates. I answered their questions and they quit pestering me. I would close my eyes, try to pass out, and they would start in again. "Come on Gary; keep your eyes open." It was really irritating. The third time this guy called Mike asked my age, he said, "How old are you again, fifty-two?" I got just raging mad and blew up. "Goddamnit, I just told you two minutes ago I was fifty-five!" That gave me another shot of adrenaline (I don't know how I had any left) and I realized I had just swore at him. I wondered how he had taken it, so I looked up at him. The sucker was grinning! I'd had first aid training for my guide's license and it came back to me then, "Come on dummy, you know you're supposed to stay awake. If you pass out, you're going to go into deeper shock." After that I quit trying to pass out.

I still had no idea how close I was to dying. They told me later they thought they were losing me a couple of times. There were times when they couldn't get a blood pressure because they couldn't find a pulse. I remember the first time I got these violent shakes through my whole body, like my muscles were all twitching. It scared me because when you see it on TV, it's supposed to be bad. I'd made it past the first one, so the second time it hit I wasn't as worried. Both Brian and the ambulance crew told me later that, although what Joanne was telling me was absolutely the correct thing to do, had I listened to her and pulled over, I would never have made it.

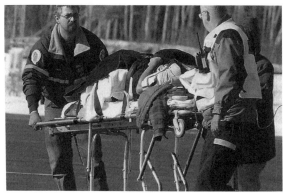

Views of the ambulance crew as they worked to save my life before placing me in the helicopter. Photos courtesy The Phillips Bee.

In the meantime, the Sheriff had called Leanne and Bill, knowing Betty was my sister. The Sheriff told Leanne that I had been in a bad logging accident. When she asked how bad it was, he just said, "He's driving himself out now." Well, how bad could it be? She knew it had to be pretty serious though, because he informed her the chopper was on its way.

We had made it to the airport, and I was just laying there with my eyes closed, waiting for the Spirit of Marshfield to arrive, when I felt a blast of cold come in as they opened the back doors. I felt a hand on my chest

and when I opened my eyes, there was Leanne on my left and my sister, Betty, on my right. No one had told them I had lost my leg. When they opened the doors it was immediately apparent what had happened. Although it hit them both hard, they sucked it up. Leanne's first thought was that she was looking at a miracle.

I opened the conversation with, "I really messed up this time." "You'll be all right," Leanne replied. "No, I REALLY messed up this time!" "You'll Be All Right!" saying it like she was trying to convince us both. That was all we said. (She said I was pretty much out of it.) It wasn't long before I could hear the chopper landing and they had to leave.

The paramedics from the chopper were Dave and Nancy. Dave got real close and said, "We're going to take good care of you." The confidence in his eyes backed up his words. He just had that look. They started an IV right away, while I was still in the ambulance. One of my rescuers told me later that he knew I was in bad shape when he saw them stick a needle in me, the size you would use on a horse, and turned the bag on wide open! Somehow, during the preparations to transfer me into the helicopter, Leanne and Dave made a connection and he told her, "We're not worried about saving his leg; we're worried about saving his life." As they were wheeling me over to the chopper, Leanne came running up and got real close, almost like she didn't want anyone else to hear, and said, "I love you." That just warmed me up inside.

Once we were in the air, I started pestering Dave for something for the pain. He kept saying, "I will, in a minute." It turns out that pain medication lowers your blood pressure even more and I had nothing to spare, although they did get me stabilized while I was in the air. I looked out the window once, just to see how high we were, otherwise I was quiet. We landed on the roof of the Marshfield Hospital, they wheeled me across to a doorway, and we bumped our way down some hallways. As we entered the operating room, there was a swarm of people waiting for me.

Someone counted one-two-three and they slid me onto a hard table. They set to work on me with their scissors and cut every stitch of clothing off, my good wool jacket included. I guess I didn't have enough energy to care this time. (When they later took my rags out to Leanne, the guy said, "We didn't think we'd ever find skin!") I felt them push a catheter in me and I knew they were going to knock me out in short order. As I lay there naked, I spotted a man who looked like he was a doctor and asked, "Will I be able to hunt again?" "Oh yes, you'll hunt again," and then I was gone.

When I came to, I was in the intensive care unit and it was after dark. I can sort of remember Leanne being there once. She said she told me that they couldn't save my leg, but I don't remember that. (It sounded like they took one look at my leg and saw that it was junk.) She wanted to spend the night with me, but they wouldn't let her. I do remember moving my leg ever so slightly and telling that it wasn't there. It hurt a lot. All night long a nurse would ask me to gauge my pain from one to ten, ten being the worst. My answers always ranged from six to eight. She explained that they couldn't give me any more pain medication because my blood pressure was too low. They had only given me five units (pints) of blood. (You know, we don't have a dipstick, so it must be hard to tell exactly how much a person really needs.) I also remember the paramedic, Dave, stopping by to check on me and leaving a black stocking cap with "The Spirit" printed on it. I wanted to tell him how much the look in his eye had meant to me, but I was so out of it, all I could do was ask him to come back. He said he would try, but he never did.

The next day, Friday, they operated again and I was given another three units of blood. The following Monday, they operated again and I got another unit. The next few days I was running a light fever, but otherwise doing all right. Wednesday evening they gave me another unit. By the next morning, my fever broke and my visitors all commented how I had gotten my color back. That final unit topped me off.

When you add them all up, that makes ten units of blood. An adult only has about twelve units in them. Obviously, I couldn't have possibly lost ten units and lived. It also seems equally obvious that they don't just let you bleed on the operating table. Being in really good shape, coupled with a cell phone and the work by my rescuers, allowed a miracle to happen that day. At the top of my medical chart my surgeon, Dr Leggon, wrote by hand, "A very heroic man!"

When I was a kid, a car hit a deer in front of our house. I watched the whole thing. As my dad and I approached her laying in the ditch, to put her out of her misery, she tried to get away. Bones were sticking out all four legs but yet she scrambled on mere stubs, trying to live. That moment has stayed with me. I know now how much I had in common with that deer. I'm surprised how that basic, primitive will to live had given me the same strength that the deer had.

During my surgery on the second day, my sister Kay was sitting with Garret in the waiting room. She was going on about how she couldn't believe I had been able to save myself. Garret's answer was matter of fact, "It doesn't surprise me; if anybody could, he could." I guess after twenty years, he had seen me do too many things the hard way. Lately, I had seen that same determination growing in him. He understood.

Don't we all wonder how we would react in a bad situation? I guess

I don't have to wonder any more, but let me tell you; it's a bad trade. I found out more about myself that morning than I ever wanted to know. I would still rather be wondering. It was all a very bad trade.

After my second surgery on Friday, they put me in a good-sized hospital room by myself. It was like they foresaw this wave of people that was about to descend on me. The Marshfield Fleet Farm (A Wal-Mart for country folk) got a lot of extra business because of me. Leanne came in, the first morning I was in there and said, "Well you made the news. Your accident was on the Tomahawk radio station." "You're kidding!" I replied. "It was just a dumb logger had an accident." I had no idea how my story would capture people's attention. The visitors were non-stop and besides wanting to wish me well, it didn't take too long before I figured out that they also wanted to hear the story. The first three or four times I told it, I got really tied up inside, but each time after that, it got easier. Only when you're lying in a hospital bed can you fully appreciate the kindness of visitors.

One visitor in particular helped me a great deal. Roger Reas was an acquaintance from the other end of the county and we had served on some committees together. He was born with a birth defect and had a fake leg. When he heard about my accident, he told his wife, "There's something I've got to do." He and his wife, Sharon, came down one afternoon and he showed me how a below the knee, fake leg worked. I made him peel everything off. I wanted to see every part. That helped me a lot, just knowing what to expect. Roger's not an acquaintance any more; he's a friend.

About the fourth day in the hospital it dawned on me that I was having a danged party! The pain medicine and all the visitors were keeping me in an unusually chipper mood. I had cried only once. I like to tell myself, when things are going bad, "The sun will come up tomorrow." It doesn't matter if the Packers are losing in the Super Bowl; it doesn't matter that your neighborhood school is going to close; it doesn't matter that your mother or brother are dying of cancer; it doesn't even matter that the President is assassinated or the Pope dies. The sun still comes up tomorrow.

I had been listening to Creedence Clearwater Revival on my headphones since 3:00 that morning, and was feeling pretty emotional. The humor from the lyrics, "There's a place up ahead and I'm goin', just as fast as my feet can fly," was not lost on me. (Those hospital beds are so tight, you cannot get those suckers rockin'.) The nurse had left the

169

drapes open just a little that morning and wouldn't you know it, my bed lined up perfectly for me to watch the sunrise. I was alive! Being able to watch the sun come up one more time really brought into focus what had almost happened. But those had been the only tears. I thought I should be depressed; this was certainly a bad deal! I was scared to death I was going to crash and I didn't want to go there.

I was seeing my surgeon later that day and I had three questions saved up for him. First, I wanted to know why there had been so little blood on the floor of my pickup. I expected to hear that your body naturally constricts blood vessels as you start to get low. He explained what had really happened was that every time my heart beat; there was less blood to pump! Whoa! My second, which were more like a group of questions, were: Would I be able to hunt again? Would I be able to ride horse again? Would I be able to log again? The answer every time was, "If you want to." When I asked him why I had been having a party and how long before I got depressed (surgeons don't handle those questions), he answered my question with another question. "Would you like to see a psychiatrist?" "You bet!"

The shrink's pretty young assistant came in first, talking to Leanne and me about my life over the years, taking notes all the while. When the psychiatrist came in later that evening, I instantly liked him. This guy was no stuffed shirt. He proceeded to tell me about myself. I liked being alone, I seldom accepted help, I was proud of who I was, self confident, determined, etc. This guy really had me pegged. He kindly kept my flaws to himself. "So what's bothering you?" he asked. "Two things." I responded. "First, I'm afraid of depression setting in and second, all these people coming in here and telling me I'm a hero is just swamping me. I don't want to be a hero. I just want to be Gary."

"Well," he said, "let's take the second one first. You are a hero. Accept it. Hardly anyone else could have done what you did. What you did was extraordinary. Most people would have died when the tree hit them. The shock alone would have killed them. Whoever was left after that would have died when the tourniquet broke. Whoever was left after that would not have been able to climb into the skidder. So you see, by the time you reached your pickup, out of 100 people, maybe two or three others would be there with you." He continued, "You survived because you are in extraordinary shape, you never smoked or drank, along with your connection with the natural world. You have experienced the brutalness and finality of the natural world firsthand; you understand

and accept that. You have learned self-reliance because you chose to put yourself in wild places where there was no one to bail you out. It's like you have been living your life to prepare yourself to survive this very moment. Your will to live was remarkable. Accept it. Another benefit to having all this company is that telling your story is really good therapy for you mentally." I nodded my head, recognizing how much easier it had become. (To this day, I have not had one nightmare about it.) "As for the depression, I would be surprised if you get depressed. Your mind doesn't work that way."

"But," he continued, "Your strengths are now a weakness. You don't know how to accept help and if you can't turn that around, your recovery is going to take twice as long. You are lying in that bed and you can't do a thing for yourself. You need to learn how to rely on others." I remember not liking that. He had just told me I was in the top four percent of tough sons-a-bitches and now I had a weakness?

As if his point had to be proven, just two and a half hours after he left, I couldn't get to sleep. I pushed the little red button and a nurse's aid came in. "I need a sleeping pill." I had been awake since 3:00 that morning and the other nights, I had not been getting much sleep either. (I'm pretty sure some of this was the drugs.) I thought she said, "I'll be right back." Well, five minutes later, no pill. Ten, then fifteen; still no pill. I was starting to steam. I set the limit at a half-hour. I actually watched the second hand go click, click, click. A half-hour and no sleeping pill!

I wasn't supposed to get out of bed by myself, but I had been to therapy, so I had a walker in one corner and a wheelchair in the other. I sat up in bed and peeled off a leg massager from my good leg, which was there to prevent blood clots. I wiggled my way down to the foot of the bed, where I could just barely reach one of the guest chairs. I slid it halfway over to the bed and hopped my butt into that one. Then I hopped my butt into another chair along the wall. From there, I could just barely reach the walker. I slid that over to me and used it to get over to the wheelchair in the other corner. I figured out how to release the brakes on that outfit and wheeled my way down the hall to the nurse's station to get my own damn sleeping pill! Do you think I could push that button one more time? I had pushed it once. I wasn't going to have to beg for help!

The nurses all gave me the look of a deer when it sees something strange. At least I had enough control not to cause a scene. I motioned to the nurse I liked the best and when she came over, I told her quietly

171

what the problem was. She also quietly told me that they were waiting for clearance from a doctor before they could give me a pill. Boy, did I feel like an idiot. She asked if she could help me back to bed, but of course I declined that too. Despite my protests, they made sure I got back into bed safely. The next day, I connected the dots and I got better at accepting help after that.

I wasn't a very good therapy patient either. I kept trying to convince them that I was one of the healthiest people in the hospital; I just had a big sore on the end of one leg. They would put this little piddly weight on my leg and ask if I could lift it ten times. Well yaa... I wanted some real weight. I knew I had a lot of work to do because I was going elk hunting in seven months and I had a logging job to get back to. There was one guy in there, named Duane, who seemed to understand. I asked for him all the time.

The drugs I was on had me wired up pretty good. The other effect they had was that it seemed everything was deeper or grander. A man poked his head in one afternoon and introduced himself. John Martwick said his wife was in the room right next to mine and he had been trying to say hi for two days, but there was always somebody else visiting. He said they lived just north of Phillips, that his wife had cancer and, when I asked, the outlook for her was pretty dim. The day after my sleeping pill performance, I got clearance to use the wheelchair, so I swung into their room to say hi. I have never seen anything like her. When she raised herself off the bed and smiled in hello, it was like I was looking at an angel. Debbie was very pretty, very calm and very kind. Her eyes just twinkled and she had this aura of goodness around her. She had everything except a halo.

A few evenings later, John poked his head in to say Debbie was being released and they were leaving. I don't know what came over me. (I think the drugs were a big part of it.) I was sitting in my wheelchair visiting with some company, so I excused myself and wheeled out into the hallway to say goodbye. Halfway out, I knew what I was going to do. I asked John to steady me as I stood up and gave his wife a hug. I told her, "I have come to understand that I was given a miracle. I don't know where it came from, why I got it, or even if I own it. But if I do own it, I want to give it to you. I don't need it anymore." I squeezed her as hard as I dared, trying to pass my miracle to her. As I pulled back, I looked into her always-smiling eyes. She simply said, "Thank you. That was very nice of you."

It turned out I didn't own the miracle and I couldn't give it away. She died a few months later. I checked around. She was truly a wonderful person. Why do good people die young? My simple answer is stuff happens. There is no rhyme or reason to why good people die and wicked, miserable people live. Stuff just happens. That philosophy helped me deal with my own accident. Rather than spend energy on things past, that I have no control over, I tend to work at things I can control. Learning from a mistake is one thing. Agonizing over and trying to find meaning in why it had to happen is another.

They initially thought I would be in the hospital for ten to fourteen days. I was actually well enough to go home on the eighth day but they couldn't find an oral pain medicine that agreed with me. On that day, I was introduced to another doctor who was going to take over my care. In a crude sort of way, it was like Dr. Leggon was a framing carpenter and Dr. Bibbo was a finish carpenter. From what I came to understand, Dr. Bibbo was instrumental in bringing this new technology, called a wound-vac, to Marshfield. It puts light suction on the wound, keeping the fluids off, decreasing the chance of infection and also increases tissue growth. Although I didn't know it until months later, their initial assessment was for an at-knee or above-knee amputation, final outcome. I knew keeping my knee was key to being able to doing the things I wanted. When I asked them what were the chances of keeping my knee that afternoon, I expected 80/20 or 90/10. I didn't like their 50/50 answer.

On the ninth day, I got to go home. During the ordeal, our neighbors had been wonderful. They had kept wood in the stove, brought firewood, snow- plowed the driveway, fed the horses and mules, fed the dogs. Their visits and phone calls continued, helping me pass the time. I knew there was no way I could ever repay their kindness, and that weighed on me for a while.

Several papers did interviews and wrote stories about my accident. Dave Carlson of "Northland Adventures", a Midwest outdoors TV program, did a nice show about me. Between all that and frequent checkups at Marshfield, I was kept pretty busy. By the third week, they determined that the end of my stump hadn't lived, so I had to go back for five days, while they cut off another three-quarters of an inch. A few weeks later, some of the tissue died right in the center, so they did a "debridement", where they cut out the dead stuff, leaving a groove in the bottom. Just when I was supposed to get a skin graft, I got MRSA, a serious kind of staph infection. Three weeks later, I finally got the skin graft to cover the groove in the bottom of the stump.

I know that the wound-vac had saved my knee, but measured from the center of my kneecap, I only had five and one-half inches of stump left. Dr. Bibbo explained that after the fourth surgery, there was not enough tissue left to pad the bones. That was going to make fitting a leg more difficult, but not to settle for anything less than a pain free prosthesis.

Dr Bibbo was a really good doctor. I enjoyed seeing him and his staff, although his nickname was "The Grumpy Italian". During one of the early checkups, a young fella took off the bandage before the doctor came in. Bibbo's nurse, Jackie, had just come in when the young guy said, "It looks real good. Who did your amputation?" Quick as a cat I said, "Dr. Soft Maple." The poor guy, you could just see him trying to put a face on this Dr. Soft Maple. Jackie busted out laughing and he got a confused look on his face. After I explained, he thought it was funny too.

I kidded the Doc about his nickname one day and he said I would be grumpy too if I had to deal with all the paperwork and insurance companies. He had become a doctor to heal people, not push pencils. As long as I had opened the door, he decided to give me a hard time right back. "I hear you're walking all over on your crutches." (I had gotten up to two miles, mostly on roads, walking around at home.) "If you ever fall and hit the end of that stump, you're going to be real sorry." I came back with, "Look Doc, the end of that leg is like carrying a gun or carrying a baby. If you slip and fall, that's the last thing you'll let hit the ground." "Well," he said, "I don't know much about guns, in fact they scare me, but I understand the baby analogy!" As long as we were having fun that day, I decided to thank him for saving my knee, that I was lucky to have gotten him. He matter-of-factly told me that it wasn't luck. He took all the hard cases.

I think there was some concern that I might let myself out of this life, although no one spoke of it. That is until one day when Mike Fromholz brought it up on one of his many visits. If you ever need a friend to cover your back, you'll want someone like Mike. A few years before, we, along with my brother Jerry, had led a charge to limit ATV access on county forest land, stirring up one heck of a hornet's nest. The motorized crowd directed their personal attacks at Jerry and me, leaving Mike frustrated that he couldn't get anyone mad at him! During my recovery, he was sitting on my couch one day and said, "I don't know what you're planning

174

to do, but I have a list of people, as long as my arm, I still intend to piss off. I can't do it alone. I'm going to need your help!" I laughed for a long time on that one.

Mike (also a logger) shared with me how he had been talking with another logging friend about my odds of going back into the woods. Our friend ventured that I would never be able to do it; the job is hard enough with two good legs. Mike responded, "Well, you don't know Gary very good then," to which our friend replied, "Well, if anybody can, Gary can." Comments like that had a way of giving me encouragement. They helped a lot.

I hadn't really thought about suicide, but there were days when I wished I had just died, especially when I was so sick from the medications. But the unbelievable amount of support my family received was just overwhelming. The best man at my wedding, Gary Chase, and his wife Cindy, from Phillips, set up a bank account for donations and everyone included a gift of money in their get-well cards. It began to feel like all those people had an investment in me and I couldn't let them down. I figured that the only possible way I could pay them back was to recover to the best I possibly could.

Towards the end of June we went hunting for an outfit to build me a leg. There were two highly recommended choices to pick from. Because of insurance constraints, Walkabout in Wausau, an hour and a half away, became the clear favorite. The first thing I told Darrell Cook, a fit thirtyish looking prosthetist, was that I needed to go elk hunting the last part of September. He said he would try. I said, "No, I have to go elk hunting." "Well then, we have a lot of work to do."

Foolishly, I had set that goal while in the hospital, not planning for such a long recovery. For added incentive, Don Burgess had mentioned my accident and my love for wild places in his column in "Bugle" magazine. He told his readers that I was, "healing at home-and planning another trip into wildest Idaho this fall." He added, "I wouldn't bet against him." I had to make it now.

It just so happened that Darrell had been on a few elk hunts himself and was planning another hunt the same time I was going. To make things even crazier, his tag was for the same Idaho hunting unit as mine! I took pictures along from time to time of my hunts and we spent quite a bit of time talking about elk. I had planned on going with a friend from Colorado, Gary Meinke, but sometime in August he came down with West Nile disease and he couldn't go. To Leanne's relief, Darrell decided he would go with me. A pack-in trip deep into a wilderness area held great appeal to him.

Dr. Bibbo had been correct; it was hard to get a comfortable fit on my leg, but Darrell was up to the challenge. I couldn't believe how weak I was, although, the first day I walked out of his office, Darrell said I was three months ahead of most of his patients. With lawn grass snagging my foot, I couldn't understand how I would ever be able to push my way through weeds or brush. Another problem I had was that, after being in a knee-immobilizer for four months, I could barely bend my knee. Insurance agreed to pay for some physical therapy from Medford Therapy and Fitness.

Luck once again came my way, when on about the fourth visit, I got a substitute therapist named Janie. The first thing Ms. Grunwald asked me was what I wanted out of these sessions. Well, I wanted to be 100 percent. She worked the heck out of me and it felt like the insurance company and I got our money's worth that day. From then on, I asked for Janie all the time. Later, I asked her about that question, because I thought it was sort of strange. She said a lot of patients reply that all they want is to go on disability. There would be no point in putting them through the torture she was putting me through. Well, okay, torture may be a little strong, but it was hard. Janie knew how to push my buttons, when she really wanted to challenge me. She'd put some weight on a machine and say, "See if you can do ten of these—Oh I'm sure you can't, just do as many as you can." Ten button popping reps later, she would act surprised and say, "You did it!" She also got my knee so I could bend it at least 90 degrees.

I was surprised how slowly my strength came back. I could see progress week to week, though. I started riding horses again, experimenting on how to make it work. I fashioned a piece of leather to cover the front of the stirrup to keep my foot from sliding through, if I fell off. My fake leg had lots of adjustments, so when I rode, I would make myself bow-legged to keep the foot from hitting trees. I had to get on the off side (right side) of my mare, but she was fine with that. I couldn't put equal weight on my left stirrup, so I hung my four-foot crosscut on that side to balance my saddle. Two months after getting my leg, I thought I was ready.

Darrell and I pulled into the Idaho trailhead twenty-eight hours after leaving home. We got a good night's sleep there and got up early enough to have the mules packed and ready to go by daylight. The twelve-hour ride in started out all right, some pain for a while, but then

176

it kind of got numb. I know the ibuprofen helped. At times, brush would catch my stirrup and push it back, pulling my fake leg out of position, which would make my whole leg throb. I finally solved that problem by tying the stirrup forward to the breast collar. The long downhills were also hard. Normally I get off and walk those stretches because the horse's gait is so stiff and jarring. My back and stomach muscles weren't strong enough to compensate for my weak leg. Gratefully, Darrell was more than strong enough to saw and chop our way up the trails and we made it into camp right at dark.

We both knew Darrell would do most of the hunting because I was limited to very short hikes. I thought I had convinced myself that just going on this trip, just being back in the wilderness, was going to be enough. One evening, staring at the mountain, I realized just being there, breathing air and taking up space, wasn't enough. I missed not being able to rise to the challenge of the mountains. I knew then that I just had to do a whole lot better, but could I? The next evening, as I was hobbling along with Darrell on the pack trail up to a meadow for his evening watch, I asked him if I would ever be able to climb the mountain again. He dodged the question by saying a lot of guys are still in a wheelchair nine weeks after getting a leg. When I persisted, the look in his eye told me I would not like the answer before he spoke, but when he added that maybe if I was twenty-five or thirty again – well that gave me the optimism I needed. Hell, in the mountains, I had always been as good as those young guys on a bad day.

My prosthetist, Darrell, and his elk – a "rare gift from those mountains."

Darrell shot a nice heavy-horned five-point that evening. Sitting alongside him, while his excitement spilled over into me, was as good as if I had pulled the trigger myself. An easy bull like that, close to the pack trail and to camp, was a rare gift from those mountains. We camped a few more days and then packed out the twenty-three miles back to the truck. It had been a good trip. I left the mountains stronger and more determined than I had arrived.

After I got home, I spent some time on the Internet, hoping to find an elk hunter who was shorter on one side, like me. I guess I was hoping that if I found another hunter, who could do it, that it would shore up my confidence. I didn't have much luck with that and after a little while I realized that it didn't much matter anyway. All I needed to do was be patient, keep doing my best and I could win, the same philosophy I had used to get to the top racing sled dogs.

I ran a short trap-line on the river that fall. Wading the river on slippery rocks was better therapy than what even Janie could have thrown at me! I hunted during deer season and was even a slight help dragging a buck out with my nephew. I made some deer drives with the crew, but had to be really selective where I went. Trail-less, swampy country was definitely out.

Staring at the montain one night, I knew this wasn't enough.

Leanne was not in favor of me going back to logging. I couldn't use my old, "I've come home to you every night" line anymore, so instead started saying, "I've made it out of the woods every time, haven't I?" The first part of December, I fired up my skidder and did a few exploratory skids around my house, cutting down and dragging up some dead elm for firewood. I did a lot of stumbling around while limbing, but I saw I could do it, if I took my time. Exactly to the day, ten months after I had crawled out of the woods, I went back in. The first thing I did, as I knew I would, was to go back and get the tree that had done its best to be a widow-maker. When I got to the spot, everything was still as it had been when I had crawled away.

I had not been able to understand why that bigger tree, which was behind, hadn't smashed down the smaller one in front, as it was falling. Looking closely now, I figured that the bole of the big one had been slightly off to the left of the smaller one, up high. It had ushed the smaller one off to the right, where its top had hung up on a big yellow birch limb. Even then, it should have smashed it down, except that there was a big knot on the limb, which snagged the top and prevented the small one from sliding off. On the other end, with the downward sliding pressure of the big one, it had actually wedged the butt of the little one on the stump, which kicked the big butt sideways, chasing me down. The whole thing had been a lot of circumstances coming together perfectly. My leg being sheared off was a result of inches and fractions of a second. Had I been a hair faster, I would have turned around and said, "Whew, that was close," and went back to work. Had I been a hair slower, I would have been nothing more than a bloody splat in the snow.

I went over to the stump where my leg had been sheared off. I dusted off the snow and could see where the butt of the big tree had come down, right on the very edge of the stump, barely taking the bark off. That's why my leg had been sheared off so clean. I suddenly started feeling really sick and had to sit down. I sat on that stump for a little while and then tears began to come. I don't know why I cried. I suppose they were tears of gladness that I had lived and at the same time tears of sadness, because I had paid a hefty price. When I finally got all that out of my system, I hooked onto that big soft maple and drug it out to the landing. I'd won; by golly, I'd won!!

While I was driving to work, a few weeks later, I was wondering why it had been so important to get that tree, first thing. Well, I knew I had to face it at some point, so I guessed I just had to get it over with. But then I also realized why it was so important to go back in the woods. I wasn't about to let the woods beat me. To quit would have been like saying I was afraid and there was no way my Edinger pride could handle that. Besides, I liked logging. Take away the bugs and the heat and the mud of summer, the bitter cold in winter, the breakdowns, the hard hours of physical work and the danger and it's a great job! Yes, I know that sounds crazy, but I grew up with all that stuff and I'm used to it. When I listen to all my friends constantly complaining about their stingy boss or their idiot co-workers or their complaining clients, I know I have it made. Logging allows me so much freedom. Where else can you bust out singing or bust out swearing any time you want? I knew I would never be able to cut as much wood as I used to, but I did want to see if I could at least make it worthwhile economically.

The plan was to take it real easy and just do what I could comfortably. I even asked Mike for some help with cutting some big red oak, which I felt were too dangerous for me to tackle. I started out slow all right, but it wasn't long before I started pushing it. One day, after I had finished limbing a skid, I sat down on a log to rest and started feeling sorry for myself. Everything I did was so hard and clumsy, my leg was hurting and I wasn't getting much production. All of a sudden, a thought came out of the air, "If you can drag your butt out of the woods with a leg sheared off, bleeding to death, you sure as hell can do this." Just like that, I took another step up. Logging was just like trapping, the best therapy you could ever ask for, and I was getting paid for it! By the end of winter, I had gotten strong enough to make it pay.

Another thing I did all winter was try to call out from that job on my cell phone. I bet I tried two dozen times and not once could I get enough signal to dial out. There was one sweet spot, where my logging road made a T intersection, where on most days, I would have to move ten feet one way or another to get it to work. On the day of the accident, I had started talking 300 yards to the north and then kept talking another 800 yards to the east of that sweet spot. Another miracle had occurred that day.

That spring of 2008, Denny Caneff, the Executive Director for The River Alliance of Wisconsin, came up from Madison to join me in a canoe run down the South Fork of the Jump. The Jump is a fast flowing stream that is only canoe-able during high water, which is usually during breakup, just after the ice goes out. It's a bit dangerous because the water is so cold. About halfway down, I picked the wrong side of a little island to go on. Once we got in there, there were some trees lying horizontally just above the surface and the current was too swift to avoid them all. When the canoe rolled, the bow and Denny were next to shore, while I was thrown backwards, upside down, into the middle of the channel. I guess, because my leg trapped so much air, my life jacket was having a fight with my leg to see which end would come up first.

Denny was standing, next to shore, immediately. The canoe was wedged upside down under the tree and for an instant, he saw my fake leg pop out of the water and thought that it had come off. I wasn't coming up and I wasn't coming up and he was just getting ready to dive in, figuring I was trapped under the canoe, when I finally popped up, far downstream.

Like I said, I was having a heck of a time getting back to the surface. The swift current was rolling me around pretty good, but what surprised me the most was how fear roared up inside of me. It was the same fear I had felt when my leg was sheared off. You would think, after what I had been through before, that anything would be a piece of cake, compared to that. Instead of being used to it, it was like I had more practice in how to feel it. When I finally broke the surface, I didn't like having to deal with that too. I still had a hold of my paddle, in my right hand, and when I spotted a tree limb reaching out over the water close to the surface, I grabbed it with my left, knowing the current would then swing me into shore.

We couldn't get the canoe loose, so we ended up with quite a hike out to the county road. I sort of knew that country, knowing once we found the logging road coming into that area, it wouldn't be too bad getting out. Denny was concerned about me walking very far, but I wasn't. We had to get the canoe out right away for a couple of reasons. Denny's car keys were in his dry bag, tied in the canoe and I figured when the water went down, my canoe would float free and head downriver.

Once on the road, we caught a ride back to my place. I called my friend Butch, just the man for the job, to come to our rescue. He and his son Jake came down with two kayaks and a canoe and we floated back down to the island. I took along a snowhook, from my dog racing days, and a long rope to use as a grapple. We managed to rescue my canoe and Denny's keys with only slight damage to the aluminum boat and my pride. The next day, I conned my neighbor, Ed Olson, into another canoe trip with me, so I could get rid of that fear. I happened not to mention that I had rolled the canoe the day before.

Three months later, we were back on schedule with our family summer pack-in trip to the mountains of Idaho. We did a lot of reading and napping and fishing on this trip and we had a great time. There is this one lake, with great fishing, that you have to bushwhack into; there is no trail. To reach it, high in a side canyon, you have to navigate a steep grade and lots of down timber. That's the lake, when Aubrey was only six, that I was having a hard time getting my own fishing pole ready because she was catching one with every cast. When I finally said that she needed

Aubrey: "I'm just a fish magnet."

181

to slow down so I could fish a little, she came back with, "I guess I'm just a fish magnet." In my mind, getting up to that lake was going to be my test. I made it and that made me feel pretty good. Later that fall, because I had promised my friend from Colorado a wilderness hunt, I took him on his elk hunt while I did the camping. He saw a few nice bulls, but they didn't cooperate.

Besides logging the following winter, I took a job teaching a logging class for our local Technical College. Starting in the fall, it ate up twenty consecutive Saturdays, but that was all right because I work almost every day in winter anyhow. I enjoyed the students, but having to deal with a boss (administrator) way over in Wausau, who I never did meet, was hard. Everything I had learned the hard way, I tried to teach them. It was all very hands on. You can't learn how to be a logger in a classroom. Towards the end, our local paper did a story on the class and I tried to get them to title it, "One-legged logger teaches others how they can become one, too!" but the reporter wouldn't bite. As far as my own production went, I was still improving.

So now I'm back to our summer trip of 2009. After the cold wet day of packing in, where we had such a tough time because of all the down timber, the weather had been great and we camped along a high mountain lake with lots of graze for the stock. After a week, we packed out of there and went back into the camp where Aubrey said she was a "fish magnet." Normally a two and a half hour ride in, it took us six hours, because of all the down timber. Paul Hopkins, a friend from the Bitterroot Valley I had met while guiding for Tommy, hiked in to spend a few days with us. The following day, we all hiked up to Aubrey's lake. After catching and cleaning enough cutthroats for a belly swelling supper, I tried a different route coming back down. I thought it would be easier, but it turned into a real mess. When we did finally reach the bottom, Leanne twisted her ankle real bad, jumping across the creek.

Let me tell you a little about Paul. When I had two good legs, I could really cover ground and he's the only guy I'd found who could out-walk me in the mountains. A little younger and a little longer-legged, he's just a hiking machine! So this one year, Paul rode us into a place he liked. After camp was set up, he and I hiked up to the top of the nearest peak that evening. He led the way, and all the way up, I stayed right with him. Standing at the top, I was feeling pretty good about how I had kept up and I told him so. He said, "Ya I know, I haven't been feeling good all year." You could hear the air go out of my balloon all the way back to Wisconsin! That's one of the things I like about Paul; he never sugar coats anything. He just says it like it is.

Leanne's ankle was still swollen the next day, so the girls stayed in camp while Paul and I hiked a pack trail up to another lake. I caught some of the biggest trout ever that day. On the way back down, while we cooled off by this little waterfall, Paul said, "You know, you can go anywhere in these mountains. Watching you yesterday, I was impressed. It may take you a while, but you can go wherever you want." I said, "Thanks, that makes me feel pretty good." "I didn't say it just to make you feel good, I really meant it." I smiled then, trying to keep my emotions in check, "I know you did, that's why those words coming from someone like you means everything. You can't imagine how much that helps me."

I've always expected a lot from people around me. I also liked being around people who expected a lot from me. I read this line one time and I liked it so much, I wrote it down. It went, "If you meet a loner, no matter what they tell you, it's not because they enjoy solitude. It's because they have tried to blend into the world before, and people continue to disappoint them." There's a lot of truth in that for me except I really do enjoy solitude for its own sake. I think what disappoints me most about others is how they quit so easily. Every time they have to put a little extra effort into a task, or things start to get a little scary, they just lay down on you. I prefer being around people who are willing to rise to a challenge; people like Paul.

Another thing I would change about the human race is our own shortsightedness. It's hard to think long term when you are raised on a steady diet of advertising, screaming for instant gratification 24/7. A person has to get off to the side, like in quiet wild places, to see humanity more clearly. I think, in the end, our basic genetic makeup of greed and shortsightedness will destroy us. No matter how smart we think we are, we just won't be able to help ourselves.

In this last year's round of hunting (2009), I did real well. I got an elk tag and hunted for myself, going way back into the same place Darrell and I had gone. It worked out for Dave Stalling, the former conservation editor for "*Bugle*", to help me with my trip. He had just moved back to Missoula from Washington, D.C., and needed to get into the mountains for a while. The mountains were not in a generous mood this time, but I did finally kill a bull five miles above camp, just about as far away as you can get from the trailhead. For some reason, this hunt was special. Unlike earlier hunts, I really wanted to get one and I think I needed to prove to myself that I could really do it. Having to work extra hard, packing him twenty-eight miles back to the trailhead in that rugged country, only added to the sense of accomplishment and the size of this bull's horns was certainly frosting on the cake.

During our deer season, I was a real help to Garret, helping him drag out his buck the first evening. Late in the season, another buck made the mistake of coming out to me during one of our drives. I also held up my end, when it came my turn to drive. Still, I'm shocked to realize how long it has taken for my strength to come back.

This last winter's logging season, I did what I thought was impossible. I cut as much wood as I had the year before I'd lost my leg. The doctors had not lied to me; I could do whatever I wanted to, they just happened to leave out the part about how hard it would be. It was very difficult and I only missed two days all winter, but still… If I can do all that, where is there any room for complaint?

BUM LEG OR NOT

So that pretty well is the story of my life. Until I wrote all this down, I had never realized how so many chance encounters had impacted my life. A perfect example is the chance encounter with Dave Stalling, which gave me the confidence that I could actually write this book. Numerous people suggested that I should get someone to write it for me, but if it was going to happen, I had to do it myself, the hard way. Writing about Mom dying, when I had just turned eighteen, also made me wonder if that changed how I lived my life. I guess there is no way to really know. When I add up all the experiences in my life, it seems like perhaps there are enough for three lifetimes. I've experienced a lot.

I've known the love of a good woman and the pride of having two great kids. I've felt the closeness of an extensive family and a few, very special friends. I've felt the bat making solid contact with the ball in a championship game, the exhilarating feeling of a world-class dog team and the heart pounding excitement of aiming at a big game animal, just before I pulled the trigger. I've known the special taste of homemade ice cream on my birthday and experienced the warm Christmases that only a house full of kids can have. I've also known the joy of learning in a one-room country school.

I've floated, in my imagination, with Northern Lights too glorious to describe, across a high arctic sky. I've known the beauty of paddling across a wild Canadian lake under a full moon and of drifting down the Yukon under the twilight of the midnight sun. I've listened to the soft whisper of my river, as fireflies twinkled to the call of a whippoorwill floating across our field on a warm summer's night. I've heard the tinkle of my lead mare's bell in a high mountain meadow on a cool summer's evening. I've listened to the magical sound of a wild bull elk's bugle, as I pulled a pack string on a frosty mountain morning. I've sucked in that wonderful breath of life-giving air, after being under the water too long and I've witnessed a sunrise I thought I would never see again. Who could ask for more?

Me, that's who! It just feels like I have a lot of living to do yet, bum leg or not. The memories have been fantastic, but I want some more. A few years back in elk camp, my nephew Tom came up with a funny line about how my tombstone would end up reading. It would say, "Here lies Uncle Gary, survived a childhood house fire, a near drowning in a summer flood, a mountain lion attack, a two-day mountain blizzard, (now add) and a tree nearly killed him. Died at the age of 92. Drowned in his bowl of oatmeal!"

I suppose dying at the breakfast table would be all right, but that sounds too easy. I'd rather be way back in the woods, so they have to work hard at getting me out. I would be extremely happy if I never have another life challenging moment, but I'm not going to quit living, in order to avoid it. Here's a line someone else made up that really hit home when I read it: "Life should NOT be a journey to the grave with the intention of arriving safely in an attractive and well-preserved body, but rather to skid in sideways-body thoroughly used up, totally worn out and screaming 'WOO-HOO, what a ride'!!"

There is an outdoors class at our high school and every year I take my horses and mules there to expose the students to another way of wilderness travel besides backpacking. In honesty it gives me a chance to preach about the value of wilderness and wild places. I tell them that if I can afford a big enough tombstone when I die, I want this famous quote from Thoreau carved on it:

"I went to the woods because I wished to live deliberately, to front only the essential facts of life, and see if I could not learn what it had to teach, and not when I came to die, discover that I had not lived."

I've spent my entire life seeing how far I could get. From the experiences motivated by those desires, I already know that I have lived; for me the final question will be, will I have lived enough!!

THE END

LISTING OF BOOKS

Additional copies of *Gary Edinger's "Will to Live: A Saga of Survival"* and many other of Stoneydale Press' books on outdoor recreation, big game hunting, or historical reminisces centered around the Northern Rocky Mountain region, are available at many book stores and sporting goods stores, or direct from Stoneydale Press. If you'd like more information, you can contact us by calling a Toll Free Number, *1-800-735-7006,* by writing to the address at the bottom of the page, or checking us out on our website at www.stoneydale.com. Here's a partial listing of some of the books that are available.

Historical, Hunting Reminisces

Hikes and Climbs to Bitterroot Mountain Summits, By Michael Hoyt. A gorgeously-illustrated, with over 300 color photographs, detailed guide for beginning and intermediate climbers to 50 mountains and 60 routes in the Bitterroot Mountains of western Montana and neighboring Idaho. 384 pages, 5½ by 8½-inch format, extra-durable softcover

Dale Burk's Montana, By Dale A. Burk. In vibrant text covering the full story of Montana and stunning color photographs, the author takes you into the heart and soul of wild Montana. 8x10-inch format, 150 color photographs. Hardcover and softcover editions.

Colter's Run, By Stephen T. Gough. A stirring novel of famous early-day frontiersman John Colter and the time he spent in the headwaters of the Missouri River, the Three Forks country, trapping, fighting with and eluding the dreaded Blackfeet Indians, all the while trying to live up to forces within himself that compelled him to face constant death. What he accomplished is legendary, that he survived that experience is miraculous. 6x9-inch format, 392 pages, softcover.

Reflections From the Golden Era of Hunting, By Fred S. Scott. As one of Idaho's most famous hunting figures, Fred Scott has pulled together 63 stories of big game hunting for elk, bear, deer and antelope as a companion book to his earlier "Memories of Hunting Idaho's Golden Era.256 paes, 6x9-inch format, softcover.

Memories of Hunting Idaho's Golden Era, By Fred S. Scott. Experience, through the stories of this book by one of Idaho's most revered big game hunters and master storytellers the saga of a lifetime spent in quest of elk, deer, bear and other game species over a lifetime spent in the wilds of Idaho. 64 chapter, many photographs, 256 pages, 6x9-inch format. Softcover.

From Cottontails to Kudu, By Mitch Rohlfs, Ph.d. The tradition of a life being shaped by the rigors, challenges and joys of hunting looms large in this book, which details the transformation of a young boy on his first rabbit hunt into an international big game hunter and accomplished upland bird hunter. 6x9-inch format, hardcover, 256 pages, dozens of photographs.

189

The Trail of a Sportsman, By Duane Bernard. Follow the author on a life-long quest to hunt big game across the world and to achieve what is called Oregon's "Super Slam" on a working man's budget. Go with him on adventures to Montana, Idaho, British Columbia, New Mexico, Alaska, Quebec, South Africa, Zimbabwe and Namibka, as well as in his native Oregon. 6x9-inch format, 154 pages, many photographs.

Cow Range and Hunting Trail, By Malcolm S. Mackay. An expanded new edition of the early-day Montana classic first issued in 1925 written by legendary rancher-outdoorsman Malcolm S. Mackay and illustrated by famed cowboy artist Charles M. Russell. 256 pages, 35 photographs, a new long-lost chapter added to marvelous stories of ranching and big game hunting in the West, this book is a reprint of a national best-seller from 75 years ago.

Copenhaver Country, By Howard Copenhaver, the latest collection of humorous stories. Contains rich humor and studied observations of a land Howard loves and the people he met along the way in a lifetime spent in the wilds. 160 pages, many photographs.

They Left Their Tracks, By Howard Copenhaver, Recollections of Sixty Years as a Wilderness Outfitter, 192 pages, clothbound or softcover editions (One of our all-time most popular books.)

More Tracks, By Howard Copenhaver, 78 Years of Mountains, People & Happiness, 180 pages, clothbound or softcover editions.

Mule Tracks: The Last of The Story, By Howard Copenhaver. As one of Montana's most revered storytellers and honored outfitters, Howard spent years leading his mule packstrings through the Bob Marshall Wilderness. Read here of his adventures, misadventures and other wild tales of mules in the wild country. 176 pages, hardcover and softcover editions.

Indian Trails & Grizzly Tales, By Bud Cheff Sr. A wonderful collection of stories taken from a lifetime outfitting in Montana's Bob Marshall and Mission Mountain Wilderness areas, by a master woodsman. 232 pages, available in clothbound and softcover editions.

Hunting Books

The Packer's Field Manual, By Bob Hoverson. Featuring use of the Decker Pack Saddle, this manual written by one of the top experts in the country will literally provide you with every detail necessary to successfully pack with the Decker Pack Saddle. 6x9-inch softcover format, 192 pages, many photographs and illustrations by Roger Inghram.

Hunting Chukar, By Richard O'Toole. This authoritative and detailed guide to hunting the West's most elusive game bird, the chukar, provides both experience and knowledge taken from 35-plus years of experience. Chapters on locating birds, tactics used in hunting them, gear, the choice and use of dogs, and many photographs. 6x9-inch format, softcover, 12 chapters and an appendix.

Solving Elk Hunting Problems, By Mike Lapinski. Subtitled "Simple Solutions to The Elk Hunting Riddle," this book, in 15 chapters and more than 80 photographs tells you now to cope with specific problems you'll encounter in the field – a hung-up bull, changes in elk behavior under heavy hunting pressure, peak rut activity, and so on. 6x9-inch format, both softcover and hardcover editions.

High Pressure Elk Hunting, By Mike Lapinski. The latest book available on hunting elk that have become educated to the presence of more hunters working them. Lots of info on hunting these elk.192 pages, many photographs, hardcover or softcover.

Bugling for Elk, By Dwight Schuh, the bible on hunting early-season elk. A recognized classic, 164 pages, softcover edition only.

A Hunt For the Great Northern, By Herb Neils. This acclaimed new novel utilizes the drama of a hunting camp as the setting for a novel of intrigue, mystery, adventure and great challenge set in the woods of northwestern Montana. 204 pages, softcover.

Ghost of The Wilderness, By James "Mac" Mackee. A dramatic story of the pursuit of the mountain lion, the Ghost of The Wilderness. A tremendous tale of what Jim MacKee went through over several seasons in his quest for a trophy mountain lion in the wilds of Montana. 160 pages, softcover.

The Woodsman And His Hatchet, By Bud Cheff. Subtitled "Eighty Years on Wilderness Survival," this book gives you practical, common sense advice on survival under emergency conditions in the wilderness. Softcover.

Outdoor Cookbooks

Camp Cookbook, Featuring Recipes for Fixing Both at Home and in Camp, With Field Stories by Dale A. Burk, Recipes included were recommended by Lena Jane Bacon, who was a professional camp cook for 45 years. Numerous recipes of nutritious, filling meals for the outdoorsman. 216 pages, comb binding.

That Perfect Batch, The Hows and Whys of Making Sausage and Jerky At Home, By Clem Stechelin. Detailed, common-sense instruction on techniques for making sausage and jerky at home from wild game or domestic meats. 116 pages, many photographs, comb binding.

Cooking on Location, By Cheri Eby. Exhaustive content for cooking on location in the outdoors, from menu planning to camp organization, meal preparation, and delicious recipies for all sorts and styles of dishes. 139 pages, color photographs and illustrations, comb binding.

Venison As You Like It, By Ned Dobson. A manual on getting the most from game meat, with over 200 recipies and instructions on using a variety of cooking methods. A remendous resource for those wanting to prepare tasty meals with venison, elk, antelope, moose or other wild game. Detailed index, softcover.

STONEYDALE PRESS PUBLISHING COMPANY
523 Main Street • Box 188
Stevensville, Montana 59870
Phone: 406-777-2729
Website: www.stoneydale.com